T0294565

"*The Ghost Road* is an informative, in
through Native America that reveals t[
al and tribal relations while highlighti
sistence and political innovation. In this broad legal and his
torical study, that reads as engagingly as a collection of essays,
Matthew Fletcher defines animus toward Indigenous cultures as
a major trope of US history apparent in wars of colonial expansion, reservation and allotment policies, and present-day battles
over tribal lands and economic agendas. Part Anishinaabe oral
tradition, part legal history, and part social commentary, *The
Ghost Road* illuminates competing moral frames behind the
actions of US government representatives, tribal government
officials, local non-Indian organizations, and Native community members. Ultimately, Fletcher advises the United States to
adopt Indigenous values of respect for others and care for the
well-being of future generations before it is too late."

—Tiya Miles, author of *The Dawn of Detroit:
A Chronicle of Slavery and Freedom in the City of the Straits*

"Matthew Fletcher writes with passion, insight and clarity.
He's also a great storyteller. *The Ghost Road* addresses some
of the greatest challenges faced by Indian people in times past
and today: anti-Indian animus, or more clearly – Indian hating.
Matthew is one of my favorite legal scholars. His analysis is
strong and his conversational style clearly conveys his themes.
This is a terrific book."

—John Borrows, Canada Research Chair in Indigenous Law,
University of Victoria Law School

"Philosophical, historical, and sobering – this gripping journey through the underpinnings of today's reality transforms
our views about discrimination in America. Professor Fletcher
creatively weaves Anishinaabe theory and narrative, law and
policy, and insightful analysis of social life. This book is for
everyone trying to understand the times we live in."

—Kyle Whyte, Professor and Timnick Chair,
Michigan State University

FOR NONIE

Text © 2020 Matthew L.M. Fletcher

Cover Design: Kateri Kramer
Cover Illustration: Elizabeth LaPensee

Library of Congress Cataloging-in-Publication Data
Is available from the Library of Congress.

ISBN: 9781682752333

10 9 8 7 6 5 4 3 2 1

Fulcrum Publishing
3970 Youngfield Street
Wheat Ridge, CO 80033
303-277-1623
https://fulcrum.bookstore.ipgbook.com

MATTHEW L.M. FLETCHER

THE GHOST ROAD

ANISHINAABE RESPONSES
TO INDIAN-HATING

FULCRUM

CONTENTS

PRELUDE

When Nanaboozhoo[1] was still an Anishinaabe[2] Benodjehn (child) under the care of Nokomis, his grandmother, a murderous giant came to their island.[3] The giant was killing everyone. Nokomis pulled out of the ground a load-bearing pole that helped hold up their lodge, put the little guy in the hole, and replaced the pole. She hid herself in the corner of the lodge. The giant came, saw no one, and moved on, killing and murdering everyone. By the time the giant had gone, Nokomis and Nanaboozhoo were the only Anishinaabe people left.

But Nokomis was old and forgetful, and she left Nanaboozhoo in the hole. For ten days, she puttered around her lodge, living her life, until she realized her grandson was missing. She pulled the pole out of the ground and there was a cute little bunny. Nanaboozhoo had fasted and meditated down there in the dark and had taught himself how to shapeshift. He stayed a cute little bunny for a time before turning back into a boy.

Nanaboozhoo and his Nokomis lived in the lodge on that island while he grew up. One night, when he was a young man, he dreamed that a Manitou (spirit) came to him and told him he was going to be great – great enough to kill that murdering giant. Nanaboozhoo asked his Nokomis to build a giant fire and cook a massive feast, far bigger than any two people would need. As Nokomis cooked, Nanaboozhoo made piles of muddy dirt from the shore of the island. From the mud he crafted the shapes of animals, in pairs – *mukwa* (bear), *mooz* (moose), *waawaashkeshi* (deer), *dabazi* (duck), *nigig* (otter), and many other creatures. With each pair of animals, Nanaboozhoo blew on them and gave them life. This way, Nanaboozhoo populated Anishinaabewaki (the world of the Anishinaabe people, literally "Anishinaabe world") with the creatures with whom they would live and upon which they would depend. He created a few extra creatures for Nokomis to cook, too, since Nanaboozhoo was planning a lengthy journey.

Nanaboozhoo built a *jiimaan* (canoe), loaded it with dried meat prepared by his Nokomis and berries from the island, and oiled it with *mukwa* grease. Nokomis used several *mukwa* stomachs as containers for additional grease. Nanaboozhoo also crafted special arrows and spears from the antlers of the *mooz* and *waawaashkeshi*. He set off into the *zaaga'igan* (lake) to seek the giant.

A *namé* (sturgeon) appeared next to the *jiimaan*. Nanaboozhoo offered the *namé* a little *semaa* (tobacco) and asked where he could find the giant, but the *namé* said he hadn't seen anything. So Nanaboozhoo promised the *namé* that he'd make him the largest, most powerful creature in the *zaaga'igan* if the fish would tell him where the giant went. The *namé* liked that idea a great deal and so told Nanaboozhoo where to find the giant. Nanaboozhoo was as good as his word, and turned the *namé* into the largest fish in the *zaaga'igan*.

Nanaboozhoo traveled all the way across the *zaaga'igan*. When he reached the other side, he walked in the direction the *namé* had pointed until he reached a massive archway. On either side were two *mukwaag* (bears). Nanaboozhoo offered them *semaa* and spoke to them in their own language, calling them Mishomis (grandfather). The *mukwaag* let Nanaboozhoo enter. They warned him that the giant could not be defeated, but that there was a soft spot on the back of his head under his braid. The *mukwaag* also told Nanaboozhoo that the world would end if the giant was killed.

Nanaboozhoo thanked the *mukwaag* and pressed on. Inside were many kinds of birds kept there as prisoners by the giant. These birds were supposed to warn the giant of any intruders, but they resented being held against their will. Nanaboozhoo offered these birds *semaa* and spoke to them in their own language, so they let Nanaboozhoo through without warning the giant.

Nanaboozhoo entered the giant's lodge, which was really more like a castle or a temple – a massive and egregiously wasteful structure. Nanaboozhoo found the giant asleep, belly full of the people and animals he had killed and eaten. Nanaboozhoo took careful aim for the soft spot, and killed the giant with one arrow. In the hole opened up by the arrow, Nanaboozhoo took the world's most beautiful colors. He brought them to the birds that had let him in and painted them in wide varieties of colors – all except the *aandeg* (crow) and *gaagaai* (raven), who had mocked Nanaboozhoo.

An *ajidamoo* (squirrel) approached Nanaboozhoo. The *ajidamoo* had known all of the Anishinaabe people from Nanaboozhoo's island that the giant had killed. The *ajidamoo* took Nanaboozhoo to the giant's secret room where he kept all the hearts of his Anishinaabe victims. They took all the hearts, placed them in a giant sack, and left the giant's lodge.

Nanaboozhoo and the *ajidamoo* boarded the *jiimaan* to return to the island. But on the way across the *zaaga'igan*, the *namé*, now enormous and powerful and apparently forgetful, swallowed them whole. Nokomis saw what had happened, and so did the birds Nanaboozhoo had freed. Nokomis caught the giant fish, and brought the carcass on shore. The birds began pecking at the giant fish until they opened up a hole. Nanaboozhoo and the *ajidamoo* exited with the bag of hearts. *Migizi* (eagle) was particularly helpful, so Nanaboozhoo rewarded the bird with what was left of his colors. It wasn't much but would never fade. And Nanaboozhoo gave talons to *migizi* so that he could catch fresh meat and never have to eat carrion again.

Nokomis prepared an enormous feast for the returning victors. The *ajidamoo* took the bag of hearts, burying each one in the graves of the dead Anishinaabe people, like a squirrel buries nuts. After the feast, Nanaboozhoo blew on the graves of his ancestors, bringing them back to life.

INTRODUCTION

Indian-hating is a murdering giant that must be defeated, I believe, with the tools the ancestors of Indian people have placed all around us to use. Indian people and cultures each have their own tools. In this book, I choose to explore the possibility of using Anishinaabe philosophies expressed in traditional stories of the Anishinaabe people.

Indian-hating has been an American obsession since long before "America" existed. Modern Indian people represent, and are products of, the near extinction of Indian people and the dispossession of Indian lands that allowed America to flourish. If Indian people had lived in greater numbers, or even had held onto the landholdings guaranteed to them in treaties and agreements with Americans going back five centuries, the United States would not exist in anything approaching its current form. It might not even exist at all. Living Indian people are reminders of that great, ongoing cataclysm of America. The United States owes its status as the wealthiest, most powerful nation in the history of the world to Indians and slaves. America owes a debt to Indians and slaves that America will never pay back in any meaningful sense. And Americans too often hate Indian people because of it.

I intend to show in this book that Indian-hating continues to define modern America as well. *Americans*, a term I use in this book to mean anyone living in the United States who is not an Indian person, have hated Indians so completely, so intensely, with such diversity of styles and methods as to almost completely eradicate them from America. The extent of injury inflicted by Indian-haters on Indian people throughout American history cannot be exaggerated.

Indian-hating is not the normally accepted phrase for the relationship between Americans and Indians. Most Americans likely believe Indian-hating to be a thing of the past, and many perhaps believe Indian-hating was never a thing at all. I suspect those of us who accept Indian-hating as a fact can agree that ancient Indian-haters were the violent and insane dregs of humanity who perpetrated murders and rapes and burnings on Indian people, long before the modern era that arose after World Wars I and II. For example, Herman Melville's Indian-hater, popularized in his nineteenth-century commentary on America, *The Confidence Man*, is a violent, drunken killer who casually shoots bullets at Indian people to rid them from the earth.[4] Similarly, Cormac McCarthy's Indian-hater in his late twentieth-century commentary on early America, *Blood Meridian*, is a violent, drunken bounty hunter who murders Indian people for coin and sport.[5] These men seem like fictionalized archetypes of American horror, but in Melville's writing the Indian-hating man was a real person.[6] In most Americans' understanding, vicious, horrible killings of Indian people by these Indian-haters ended before the World Wars. Now, Indian people are American Indians, and they are American citizens. The killings are over. So, too, must be Indian-hating, right?

No. Indian-hating is alive and well. The only difference between the Indian-hating of ancient America and that of modern America is the thin veneer of the rule of law. Absent a federal government that now respects the federal–tribal trust relationship (usually), there would be little or no Indian land. Absent a federal judiciary that respects the federal–tribal trust relationship (usually), there would be no tribal sovereignty. Absent federal and state prosecutors and police, there would be far more violent crime committed against Indian people. Indian landholdings are always under attack. Tribal powers are always criticized and mocked. Indian people (the lucky ones anyway) are barely a half step from a beating or a sexual assault. Indian-hating is the norm in the United States. Only unequal and inefficient rule of law enforced by American government bars a return to the ancient forms of Indian-hating – massacres, slavery, thievery, rape, arson, and other indiscriminate horrors perpetrated on Indian people.

Indian-hating also exists because of who Indian people are in addition to what Indian people represent. Indian people are people who often believe in the connection between all people and all things. Indian people are often people who understand that their actions will have expected and unexpected consequences. Indian people are often people who do not, and cannot, compartmentalize their observations of the world. Indian people are often people who accept personal responsibility for their actions. Indian people are often people who accept limitations on their personal freedoms and prerogatives in favor of the greater good.

Conversely, Americans are often people who easily compartmentalize their actions and the impacts their actions have on other people. Americans are often people who make every effort to avoid responsibility for the negative consequences of their actions. Americans are often people who are hyperindividualistic. The one thing Americans will always have in common with each other is freedom, the freedom to do what they want, no matter the consequences to others.

Not all Indian people fit my description of Americans, but many do. Indian people are Americans, after all. Not all Indians fit my description of Indians, either. And not all Americans fit my description of Americans, but many do. This book is not intended to judge or generalize about any specific group of Americans or Indians based on my subjective observations. No. In general, I derive my arguments from the written, published word. But I do depend on two assumptions that many Americans and Indian people can agree upon. The first is that modern Americans in the twenty-first century, who are often bitterly divided over even the most minor political questions, can agree on one thing – individual freedom. The second is that the one political theory that many Indian people can agree on is the theory of the seventh generation, that every major decision made by Indian people and Indian nations should be made in light of its impact on the next seven generations. These two political theories are almost complete opposites. In my view, unless Americans buy into Indian political theory, the United States will lead humanity into the abyss.

But this will not be easy. Americans hate Indians.

The ideas Indian people often espouse and the history Indian people represent virtually guarantee that Americans will hate them. Indian-hating is more than a grizzled, bearskin-wearing, shotgun-toting wild white man riding the trails of the Old West, collecting scalps of

Indian people. Indian-hating is subtle, often unnoticed – even invisible, at times, to Indians themselves. Modern Indian-hating is casual overt racism. It is environmental injustice. It is human trafficking. It is a joke about casinos. It is a corporate meeting where men "powwow." It is a college-aged woman dressed as a "Pocahottie." It is the Atlanta Braves and the Cleveland Indians and the Chicago Blackhawks and the Florida State Seminoles. And their cheerleaders, their tomahawk chops, their faux-Indian theme music, their mascots. It is the president calling a political opponent "Pocahontas." It is box-checking on college admissions. It is underfunding of Indian affairs programs. It is the US Supreme Court. It is the Department of the Interior. It is state electoral rules. It is literary fraud. It is everywhere.

A NOTE ON ANISHINAABE PHILOSOPHY

On one hand, this book is a project to assess the state of Indian-hating in American history, then and now. But it is also a project designed to reintroduce Anishinaabe philosophical thought to twenty-first-century Anishinaabe people and others interested in American Indian philosophy generally. I am indebted to Wenona Singel, John Borrows, Heidi Stark, and Dale Turner – Anishinaabe scholars whose work inspired my methodology.

Readers will soon discover that each of the chapters herein begins with an Anishinaabe story, or an *aadizookaan*. I am hoping to show to others how the lessons or teachings from our ancient and traditional *aadizookaan* have utility in the modern day. More specifically, I hope to show how Anishinaabe people can contextualize Indian-hating, to defeat Indian-hating with tools drawn from their own traditions and philosophy.

Anishinaabe political thought is at least partially rooted in Mino-Bimaadiziwin (literally, the act of living a good life). Beings acting in accordance with Mino-Bimaadiziwin acknowledge and respect all animate and inanimate things, acknowledge that all things are interconnected, and acknowledge that good and bad actions have impacts on all things. Eva Petoskey, a citizen of the Grand Traverse Band of

Ottawa and Chippewa Indians, and a former vice chair of the Grand Traverse Band Tribal Council, described the concept in more detail:

> There is a concept that expresses the egalitarian views of our culture. In our language we have a concept, *mino-bimaadziwin*, which essentially means to live a good life and to live in balance. But what you're really saying is much different, much larger than that; it's an articulation of a worldview. Simply said, if you were to be standing in your own center, then out from that, of course, are the circles of your immediate family. And then out from that your extended family, and out from that your clan. And then out from that other people within your tribe. And out from that people, other human beings within the world, other races of people, all of us here in the room. And out from that, the other living beings... the animals, the plants, the water, the stars, the moon and the sun, and out from that, the spirits, or the *manitous*, the various spiritual forces within the world. So when you say that, *mino-bimaadziwin*, you're saying that a person lives a life that has really dependently arisen within the web of life. If you're saying that a person is a good person, that means that they are holding that connection, that connectedness within their family, and within their extended family, within their community.[7]

Mino-Bimaadiziwin informs individual Anishinaabe life choices but also forms the basis for Anishinaabe *inaakonigewin* (law). Fred Kelly, an Anishinaabe and citizen of the Onigaming First Nation in Canada, draws the connection between Mino-Bimaadiziwin and Anishinaabe legal principles:

> The four concentric circles in the sky – *Pagonekiishig* – show the four directions, the four stages of life, the four seasons, the four sacred lodges (sweat, shaking tent, roundhouse, and the Midewe'in lodge), the four sacred

drums (the rattle, hand, water, and big ceremonial drum), and the four orders of Sacred Law. Indeed, the four concentric circles of stars is the origin of the sacred four in *Pimaatiziwin* that is the heart of the supreme law of the Anishinaabe. And simply put that is the meaning of a constitution.[8]

Mino-Bimaadiziwin is both a worldview and a goal. It is both spiritual and secular. Many Anishinaabe people believe that Mino-Bi-maadiziwin, living a good life, is a goal that can be achieved through the acknowledgment of the interconnectedness of all people and living creatures. Many other Anishinaabe people believe Mino-Bimaa-diziwin can only be achieved through the assistance and cooperation of *manidowaag*, the spirits. While perhaps to some Anishinaabe people it may be folly for us to discuss and analyze Mino-Bimaadiziwin in a purely secular manner, I come to this work as a legal scholar, not a religious practitioner.

I think of Mino-Bimaadiziwin as a kind of fundamental law, the guiding principle of all traditional Anishinaabe people. The notion of living a good life is a bit vague for legal analysis, but just fine for philosophical work. Helpfully, there are more principles that derive from this guiding principle.

Mino-Bimaadiziwin is, for many Anishinaabe people, the origin of the Niizhwaaswii Mishomis (or) Nokomis Kinoomaagewinawaan (Seven Grandfather or Grandmother teachings), that encompass the core teachings of the Anishinaabeg: Nibwaakaawin (Wisdom), Zaagidwin (Love), Manaadjitowaawin (Respect), Aakodewin (Bravery), Gwekowaadiziwin (Honesty), Dibaadenizowin (Humility), and Debwewin (Truth). Anishinaabe elder, teacher, and leader Edward Benton-Benai introduced the Seven Grandfather teachings to a modern audience in the 1970s:

1. To cherish knowledge is to know WISDOM.
2. To know LOVE is to know peace.
3. To honor all of the Creation is to have RESPECT.

4. BRAVERY is to face the foe with integrity.

5. HONESTY in facing a situation is to be brave.

6. HUMILITY is to know yourself as a sacred part of the Creation.

7. TRUTH is to know all of these things.[9]

The Seven Grandfathers, in this telling, were seven powerful *manidowaag* that wished to help the Anishinaabeg long ago when times were much tougher. They sent for an Anishinaabe person to hear their teachings and bring them back to the Anishinaabeg. They chose an infant to impart their teachings. The lessons were so long and complicated that the infant was an old man by the time he returned to the Anishinaabeg to impart the teachings, described as gifts. Anishinaabe scholars have tied Niizhwaaswii Mishomis (or) Nokomis Kinoomaagewinawaan to Anishinaabe religion,[10] bioethics,[11] education,[12] environmental ethics,[13] literary theory[14] – and, of course, law.[15]

The Seven Grandfathers or Grandmothers have also been referred to as part of Gagige Inaakonige, or eternal natural law. The teachings are part and parcel of the Anishinaabe way of life, values, customs, traditions:[16]

> You are being taught respect, patience, conservation . . . you are taught to give tobacco, you are taught to give something in order to take something, you are being taught a balanced way of living . . . you were taught how to share, how to care, how to be a community. . . . And that's what we were being taught from when we were living our life as little babies when we are born to how ever old we are today. These are the values. These are our customs. These are our traditions that are being taught and that were being taught. And that's how I know in my heart, when we were raised that way in our environment back home, we were actually being trained or being taught many things to become those Elders when we get older; to take our place at that circle where the Elders

sit and to understand why we were being taught these things. In that time we had no name for what we were being taught. We never said Ojibwe custom, Ojibwe way. Other people put those labels to us. What we talk about, the Elders, myself, when we talk about it, we talk about a natural process. That's why we call it Gagige Inaakonige. It's an eternal law, a natural law, everything stems from that. That's why we don't call it Ojibwe Natural Law, it's a natural law. So when we were brought up that way, to think naturally instead of putting a label to it, we get out of labeling things.[17]

And then there are seven Anishinaabe Doodeminaan (clans) – Giigoon/Meshike (fish/turtle), Waawaashkeshi (deer), Waabizheshi (marten), Ajijaak (crane), Maang (loon), Bineshinh (bird), and Mukwa (bear). Under traditional Anishinaabe *inaakonigewin*, the clans enforced the law against individual lawbreakers.

It may seem a contradiction for me to place a label on these principles when the Anishinaabe elders upon whom I rely probably would resist my labels. I'm not trying to label anything, not really. Not in this book. (When I begin my future project, the treatise on Anishinaabe jurisprudence, no promises.)

Here, I am hoping to introduce the terms and ideas I explore in this project, so that further in if I forget to explain them, readers can refer to this section.

Readers will also discern that there is no one or conclusive way to spell words in Anishinaabemowin (Anishinaabe language). I try to use the same spelling of important words and phrases I use in my own text, but I will not correct the published writings of others, because other spellings are probably not incorrect. I depend heavily on the *Ojibwe People's Dictionary*, an indispensable online resource managed and housed by the University of Minnesota.

PART 1

ANCIENT INDIAN-HATING

1

THE FRAMERS OF THE SECOND AMENDMENT

Like superheroes, every nation, religion, people has an origin story. The origin story of the Great Lakes Anishinaabeg is incredibly complicated, including the opening moments of the universe;[18] the first person, who was a demigod; a supernatural spirit named Nanaboozhoo;[19] a bunch more firsts; a great flood; and the migration of the Anishinaabeg from Wabanaki (dawn land) to the Great Lakes, or Anishinaabewaki.[20] For our purposes here, I am interested in the great flood.[21] In that part of the story, Nanaboozhoo and his brother, Mai'ingan (wolf), are among the only creatures on earth. They join together to hunt, but they are too successful. They overhunt the territory, blood flows everywhere, and their hunting terrorizes all the other creatures. The other animals meet to plan a response and decide to ask Michibizhii, the underwater panther monster, to stop Nanaboozhoo and Mai'ingan. And so Michibizhii kills Mai'ingan. Nanaboozhoo, in revenge, then kills Michibizhii. The animals, escalating this terrible conflict in return, flood the world, killing everything. Revenge nearly undoes the world. Nanaboozhoo is able to climb aboard Miskwaadesi (painted turtle) along with a few other creatures to ride out the flood. Much time passes, and it becomes clear that the water will not recede before they all starve. Miskwaadesi promises that if Nanaboozhoo can acquire some soil, he may use Miskwaadesi's back to create an island from the soil. Many animals perish swimming down into the waters seeking soil. Only the most humble of the creatures, the Wazhashk (muskrat), is able to return with a tiny bit of soil. Nanaboozhoo uses the soil to create an island on the back of the turtle, and the animals are saved. Turtle Island, known by many Great Lakes Indians as Michilimackinac, remains part of the core of Anishinaabewaki.

The origin story of the United States is a story of throwing off the oppression of the British Crown and setting a course of personal freedom for American citizens. American schoolchildren are taught about the discovery of America by Christopher Columbus, the Declaration of Independence, the Revolutionary War, the Battle of Yorktown that ended the Revolution, and manifest destiny. As any person of color knows, there is a lot left out of this origin story, most notoriously slaves and American Indians. The origin story of the United States is as mythological as the origin story of the Anishinaabe people.

American constitutional legal theory is also mythological. The story of the framing of the US Constitution is taught by law professors, myself included, as a massively important moment in legal history. Most law professors then turn to the cases, the doctrines announced and applied by the Supreme Court, interpreting the Constitution. It's what's on the bar exam. But the origin story of the US Constitution as described by the Supreme Court, that which we law professors teach, is deeply mythological. The promise of equality for all persons was pure myth. For example, few, if any, of the white men in power in America at that time, let alone any of the Framers, would have supported the suffrage for women, people of color, Indians, LGBTQ persons – anyone other than themselves. The Constitution was designed to protect, perhaps grudgingly but still very effectively, the institution of slavery. Slavery is a subject that is rarely discussed by American law professors in much detail; for too many, it is over and therefore irrelevant. Talking in a classroom about the very real legacy of slavery makes teachers and students alike very uncomfortable. It invites guilt and defensiveness. It invites anger and fear. Perhaps worst of all, a candid discussion about the way slavery dominated America during the framing of the Constitution invites critical thinking, which does not fare well on the bar exam, a test that favors memorization. When law teachers do discuss it, they rely predominantly on the story of slavery as told by white legal scholars, with a smattering of critical race theorists. Some law teachers don't even assign writings by people of color in their classes on race and the law. Until the 1980s or so, the academy relied *exclusively* on white and male scholars. Richard Delgado showed that the academy back in those days wouldn't even cite African-American, Latinx, or other minority law scholarship, ostensibly because their writings were not "elegant" enough.[22]

The Constitution was also designed to protect the nascent American nation and its citizens from Indians and Indian tribes. Indians are almost never discussed in American constitutional law courses, let alone in any detail. There is a small cohort of scholars, many of whom are Indian people, who write in the area of Indian law and policy.[23] But far less than half of American law schools even offer an Indian law class regularly. Perhaps as few as a dozen law schools annually offer multiple Indian law classes. Ask any law professor or law school administrator at an American law school that doesn't harbor an Indian law program, and they will tell you either it isn't necessary at their institution or they can't afford it. If it isn't apparent to readers now, it should be sooner or later, that the primary tool of combating Indian-hating in the United States is education. These enlightened institutions and the scholars that populate them might not hate Indians, but sadly they will do little or nothing to educate their students – an education absolutely necessary to prevent and stop Indian-hating.

One of the reasons I believe most law scholars don't take Indian law seriously, or even civil rights law, is because the most well-known theory of constitutional interpretation is originalism. Originalism is the theory that holds the Constitution's provisions must be interpreted in accordance with the original public understanding of the people of the United States as of the date of its ratification. Living constitutionalism allows for the interpretation of the Constitution's provisions to change depending on new circumstances. I went through college and law school assuming judges interpreted the law in light of the modern world, which I suppose made me accept living constitutionalism and is the mortal theoretical enemy of originalists, without even knowing there was a name for it. Most American citizens have never heard of either of these theories, let alone understand what they mean. The judges on the Supreme Court have no meaningful obligation to adopt or apply either theory in any given case, and they do wander a bit in their thinking. Still, years ago, one Supreme Court justice admitted that "we are all originalists."[24] Conservative legal scholars often claim that it takes a theory to beat a theory.[25] Living constitutionalists don't seem to be very interested in using their theory to beat originalism, or even admitting they are living constitutionalists, whatever that is. What's interesting about originalism being the preeminent theory, to the extent that there is such a thing in the court, is that it's a theory that champions the Framers. And the Framers were slaveholders and Indian-haters. They wrote a Constitution designed to maintain slavery and destroy Indians. As is likely obvious by now, originalists tend to be political conservatives.

Guns are a lightning rod for conservatives, and for originalists. At a recent talk at the University of Arizona's law school, Noam Chomsky questioned the intellectual honesty of the lead opinion in *District of Columbia v. Heller*,[26] the Supreme Court decision authored by Justice Antonin Scalia holding that the right to bear arms is an individual right, an opinion undermining the legal authority for American governments to ban guns. A real originalist, Chomsky suggested, would have looked further into the true reason for the right of militias to bear arms, which was of course to control slaves and to kill Indians. Chomsky wondered if those reasons had any import in the modern era and whether originalists would address those concerns. Of course, they do not. Or should not. Slavery and Indian killing are no longer legitimate American policy points.

Slavery aside (and that's a very fraught statement, I realize), Indians in the *Heller* opinion are conspicuously absent.[27] I am in agreement with Chomsky that a real originalist would have peppered his or her discussion of the Second Amendment with Indians. If European colonists and American pioneers had developed a horror movie industry, most of the films surely would have been about Indians, and the rest, probably, about slave rebellions. From the establishment of the earliest colonies on the Atlantic coast in the early sixteenth century until well into the twentieth century, Indian people were amongst the most terrifying beings for colonists. From the perspective of a colonist, Indians were strange, mysterious creatures. Colonists believed Indians lived in the woods, in the mountains, in the dark, everywhere. They were incredible hunters and trackers, known to be able to travel soundlessly and invisibly. Colonists believed Indians to be pagans, heathens who didn't follow a code of behavior and conduct, and that they were not civilized Christians. Indians were capable of anything, any horror. For most colonists, no ethics guided Indians. Indians were savages, cannibals, torturers.

For Indian people, these European colonists, these outsiders and strangers, were just as strange and mysterious. These colonists worshiped their belongings, they hoarded resources, they drugged themselves constantly, and they stank. These colonists often kept their women overprotected and weak, they harshly regimented their children's lives, and they were casually and viciously violent. Colonists were capable of anything, any horror. For Indians, no ethics guided these colonists. They were savages, cannibals, torturers.

The story about guns in American cannot be completely told without addressing how colonists and Indians viewed each other. An objective third-party observer might note that one key difference between these two groups during the period leading up to the founding of the American Republic was an obsession with possessions. Colonists seemed to be extremely interested in the resources that Indians possessed – food, water, land, knowledge, and, much later, timber, minerals, petroleum. The colonists had the advantage of immunity from disease and, for a time, technology. What they didn't possess at first were the resources controlled by Indian people. The colonial nations had a plan to acquire those resources, especially that resource those nations treated as completely dispensable and limitless: people.

So the colonists arrived in waves, waves upon waves. Dutch, Portuguese, English, French, Spanish, German, and other European nationalities. In the Great Lakes area, we mark time by the arrival of the big three: first the French, then the British (and now Canadians), and the Americans. The Great Lakes Anishinaabeg distinguished the goals of the French, British, and Americans by the names (or epithets) they assigned to each wave of invader. They called the French *wemitigosh*, or "men who wave sticks." They called the British *zhaganash*, an old word for "weapon" literally meaning "people who rise from the mist." Notably, the French did not seek to displace the Anishinaabe but tended toward trade and economic exploitation, sometimes through intermarriage. Many Anishinaabe today are descendants of these first French traders. The British were worse than the French, demanding more political, economic, and military fealty. But the Americans, who overtly sought to displace and even exterminate the Anishinaabeg, they called *chmookmon*, or "long knife." The Americans were the worst of all of the colonizers. Western Great Lakes Indians generally sided with the French against the British and Americans in the French and Indian War–era wars, including Pontiac's War in 1763. They sided with the British during the American Revolution and the War of 1812. The Anishinaabeg resisted the American quest to control the region well into the nineteenth century. As late as the 1840s, Michigan Indian leaders, *ogimaag*, continued to meet with the British in Canada in order to maintain a political relationship with the Crown to counteract the trespasses of the United States and its citizens – what Lewis Cass complained about in 1840.[28] The Great Lakes Anishinaabeg had much to fear from the Chmookmon leadership, people like Cass and his boss, Andrew Jackson, the American president responsible for the Cherokee Trail of Tears, the Potawatomi Trail of Death, and other acts of genocide. Americans had much to fear from Indian people, too.

Long before the American Revolution, European-descended colonists carried guns to defend themselves from Indian attack. The colonies often mandated that colonial men carry guns to provide a line of defense from Indians. But most early colonists were poor and desperate adventurers who could not afford to purchase and maintain guns. They were very expensive. So the colonies themselves usually had to provide the guns. Colonial governments and companies owned and maintained the guns for communal defense from the terrifying Indians. Famously, there are colonial laws, notably in Maine and Virginia, requiring men to bring guns to church in case of Indian attack. Some of the first gun control laws in colonial America were designed to keep guns from Indians. Fear of Indian attack must have been pervasive. They say that prior to the mass deforestation of North America, a squirrel could have traveled from the Atlantic Ocean to the Mississippi River without touching the ground, there were so many trees. America was a dark continent, full of mortal horrors like wolves, bears, and Indians, to paraphrase Supreme Court justice Anthony Kennedy in the *Heller* oral argument.[29]

By the time of the framing of the Constitution and the Bill of Rights, Americans possessed the Atlantic coast from Maine to South Carolina – the thirteen original states. Those states had boundaries, recognized by the United States and at least nominally by the international community, that reached as far inland as the Appalachian mountain range. But many of those original states did not have actual sovereignty over much of their own territories. Indian nations in Maine, New York, Pennsylvania, North Carolina, Georgia, and elsewhere controlled, or at least contested, wide swaths of American land. The United States' first treaties with Indian nations, during the American Revolution, involved these tribes located within the colonies. The treaties, notably the Treaty of Fort Pitt with the Delaware Nation,[30] were implicit acknowledgment that the United States had little power over these Indians within the borders it claimed. In that treaty, the United States dangled the promise of statehood to the Lenape Nation in exchange for peace during the Revolution and the permission to send American soldiers through Lenape territories. Americans on the frontier, even within the original thirteen colonies, anywhere near the woods where there might be Indians, carried guns for self-defense.

Moreover, Indians completely controlled the western lands, which might have seemed like alien country to most Americans. Wealthy American colonists in the East drove poor American colonists west as a vanguard to open up the western lands. They invested countless sums in land speculation, completely illegal transactions. Both the British Crown in 1763 and the US Congress in 1790 banned Americans from buying Indian lands without the consent of the national government.[31] But virtually every American of wealth in the founding generation possessed illegal property interests in the western lands. Moreover, the colonies usually promised lands in the West to American men to fight the British (and some Indians) during the Revolutionary War. The colonies and colonists owned a massive debt, with the western lands as the collateral. Of course, the biggest problem is that those lands did not belong to the Americans.

Eric Kades and Terry Anderson, legal historians with an economic methodological bent, have separately claimed that the founding generation chose the most efficient way to open up these lands, which was to send poor and desperate Americans into the woods, ostensibly to settle the land, clear property, and push out the Indians with capitalism, Christianity, and civilization.[32] Of course, these poor, desperate Americans would be killed indiscriminately by the Indian people upon whose lands they were quite plainly trespassing. So in response, the colonizer would have no choice but to arm the colonists to fight Indians. For scholars like Kades and Anderson, this was a rational political act. Indian attacks on American citizens in the western lands, if awful enough, would justify federal military intervention to protect these trespassers from harm, and for revenge. Consider the Northwest Indian War, a ten-year bloodbath in the Ohio River Valley from 1785 to 1795.[33] The war started with multiple disasters for the American army and ended with a catastrophic disaster for the Ohio River Valley Indians. The war, of course, was an experiment in blood. Send in well-armed Americans with promises of finders-keepers to either make peace somehow with the Indian people whose lands they were effectively trying to steal, or start a war. The Northwest War was the worst-case scenario arising from the federal government's early Indian affairs policy. But conflict dominated all of the borderlands between the original states and the western lands. In fact, pushing the poorest and most desperate Americans west to Indian country created bloody chaos. The chaos killed Indians and poor Americans en masse but paved the way for wealthy Americans to profit from the chaotic aftermath. This was American policy. And it required Americans to possess guns.

Yes, there is plenty of evidence that the Second Amendment was designed to allow Americans to defend themselves from the abuses of the British Crown and perhaps other invaders. There is also plenty of evidence that the Second Amendment was designed to preserve slavery as an American institution. But long before the colonists worried about British invasions and slave revolts, they worried about Indians.

Noam Chomsky's critique of theories of American constitutional originalism might or might not hit home for legal thinkers. But the historical origins of the Second Amendment surely involve the fears of Indian attack that early Americans harbored. The *Heller* decision modernizes the Framers' public policy choices, if originalism is to be believed. If the text of the Second Amendment is unchangeable, as an originalist, even a faint-hearted one like Justice Scalia, must agree, then the reasons for the adoption of the Second Amendment also cannot have changed. To be fair to Scalia, those reasons are irrelevant. But to the rest of the *Heller* majority, Justice Kennedy, for example, who does not always limit himself to the text alone, public policy reasons matter. Justice Kennedy and the rest of the majority might be persuaded by the original policy reasons, or by twenty-first-century policy reasons. Justice Kennedy, after all, is an architect of Eighth Amendment jurisprudence that allows the federal judiciary to take into consideration evolving standards of decency in making judgments about cruel and unusual punishments.[34]

Let's examine the originalist public policy reasons. Scalia was famous in statutory interpretation law circles as one who *always* refused to consider the deliberative statements members of Congress made when debating bills, or what lawyers call the legislative history of a statute. But as an originalist he might, without irony, consider seriously the legislative history of a constitutional provision. The legislative history of the Constitution is vast, contradictory, and a complete mess. There's the history of the framing, the super-secret Constitutional Convention, written and rewritten secretly and cryptically by James Madison. Then there's the history of each of the ratification debates at each of the original thirteen states, much of which came from commentaries in newspapers and magazines. And there's the understanding of what the Constitution meant in the First Congress – that esteemed group of policy makers were the first official interpreters of the Constitution, so they should know. Don't forget the US Supreme Court, either. Of course, all that history comes exclusively from propertied and moneyed white men. The originalists now refer to the "original public understanding" of the Constitution as the keystone. But the "public" of that characterization is such a small portion of the actual American public as to be comically warped. No one really knows for sure, no matter what those confident alpha male historians and lawyers say, what parts of the legislative history are important. And for some reason, no originalist wants to believe that perhaps that legislative history should be completely irrelevant in the twenty-first century. When ideology confronts historiography, ideology always prevails. And an originalist like Scalia might be tempted to take disparate and discrete statements as *law*.

In *Heller*, Scalia doesn't do much that would make an originalist proud. He reads the text in a vacuum, linguistically, an exercise that might have been just as interesting to Chomsky, the world's current leading linguist. Scalia does detain himself on public policy and history with an extensive review of the concerns of Englishmen about losing their guns, a circular argument that seemingly concludes that the English wealthy elite had guns in order to prevent their government from taking their guns. If the English, then so, too, Americans. Scalia apparently did not want to emphasize the need for Americans to keep guns for the protection of the nation in case of invasion by a foreign power. To do that would allow for some pretty severe regulation of guns, the kind of regulations that many of the colonies imposed. Imagine if the District of Columbia's handgun ban allowed for an exclusion of District residents to use their weapons only if the British invaded D.C. Lot of good that did in the War of 1812, incidentally, when the Capitol and the White House burned. (In the scoreboard of wars with our neighbor to the north, America is losing one to nothing.)

What Scalia simply refused to discuss was that Americans primarily needed guns to keep down slaves and to kill Indians. From the perspective of a modern Indian person reading the opinion (and likely equally applicable to a descendant of slaves as well), Scalia's opinion is a complete non sequitur, a sleight of hand. When Scalia does mention Indians or slaves, he does it to make a clever if disingenuous rejoinder to his white colleagues on the court. Citing postenactment authorities limiting freed Black people's right to bear arms, Scalia mocked the *Heller* Court's liberal-moderate dissenters for suggesting that their interpretation of the amendment, which would allow D.C. to ban handguns, unintentionally supported race-based restrictions on guns. Scalia seemingly says that if any American jurisdiction could ban handguns, they would do it to keep guns out of the hands of people of color. And that's why the Second Amendment could not be intercepted to allow handgun bans.

Some of the Court's amici (or "friends of the court," people or entities that file additional briefs to provide greater context to the court in important cases), such as the Pennsylvania Senate, were more explicit in discussing Indians and slaves, citing the colonists' fear of Indian attack as justification for the Second Amendment.[35] According to the Pennsylvania Senate of the 2000s, the Pennsylvanians of the founding generation had every reason to fear Indians. The state was heavily forested and full of Indian people, which was the reason the first United States–Indian tribe treaty was the Treaty of Fort Pitt, where the United States attempted to secure a military alliance with Indians in 1778. It is telling that of the dozens of amicus briefs supporting the Second Amendment's broadest interpretation, no one wanted to talk about Indians and slaves. Slavery is over. So there is no reason to worry about slave revolts. Indians attacks are over, too. So are the depredations of the British and the hated Canadians. The United States possesses and deploys the largest, most powerful military in the world's history. There will be no invasion of American soil. If we all die in war, it'll be from nuclear or chemical attack. Our guns won't help us then.

If Scalia had been willing to take seriously the issue of slavery and Indians, then his argument might not have been so implausible. The argument also would have been revealed for its bigotry underlying the claim to gun rights. In order to win, Justice Scalia had to frame the Second Amendment more generally, to make it more about the average American in the twenty-first century rather than about slavery and Indian history. Scalia won this battle, but something tells me the war over the interpretation isn't over, and *Heller*'s days were numbered even as Scalia was reading the opinion aloud in the Supreme Court chambers. The opinion was bullshit, in the way that philosopher Harry Frankfurt meant it, reckless disregard for the truth, told primarily to influence people already predisposed to support gun rights.[36]

American guns are about wealthy people in power controlling poor people of color. *Saturday Night Live*'s Michael Che argued (as a joke) that the best way for America to restart the political movement for gun control is for brown people to start carrying guns with the same vigor as white men. Hell, even the killings of dozens upon dozens of schoolchildren isn't enough to persuade Congress to strengthen federal gun control laws, although we should all be delighted if the young people's movement that began in Parkland, Florida, bears fruit (not arms).

The Second Amendment doesn't mention Indian country. The US Constitution generally doesn't apply to Indian tribes. Tribes were not invited to the Constitutional Convention. Tribes were not invited to ratify the Constitution. There is nothing in the Constitution that would allow Indian tribes to ratify it and join the federal–state alliance established in it. Tribes could ban guns. In 1968, Congress enacted the Indian Civil Rights Act, which extends via statute (also known as the Indian Bill of Rights) many federal civil rights to persons under tribal jurisdiction.[37] Congress did not provide a right to bear arms to Indians, who are usually the people under tribal jurisdiction. Congress amended portions of the Indian Bill of Rights in 1986, 2010, and 2013; the latter two amendments came after *Heller*, from a Congress generally dominated by the Republican Party. Still, no right to bear arms. Congress might be deferring to Indian tribes, letting tribal governments make the decision on tribal citizen gun rights – or maybe ensuring the rights of people of color to possess guns just isn't in the interest of Congress.

Maybe it's too much to make hay over the fact that Congress doesn't seem interested in guaranteeing Indian people under tribal jurisdiction the right to bear arms, at least to the extent guaranteed to people under federal jurisdiction in *Heller*. Indian tribes aren't doing much to either protect or restrict the right of their citizens to bear arms, excepting those tribes with tribal members who are limited in the exercise of their treaty hunting rights by federal and state laws banning felons from possessing guns.

Perhaps the real story here is how Indian tribes deal with twenty-first century gun violence. Jim Diamond, a lawyer from Connecticut who was deeply affected by the Sandy Hook killings of twenty schoolchildren and six adults in 2012, compared the American response to mass gun violence to how the Red Lake Band of Chippewa Indians dealt with it in 2005, when nine people were killed on the Red Lake Indian Reservation in Minnesota.[38] Diamond saw many commonalities in the political response to mass killings outside of Indian country. Two commonalities are important: (1) the perpetrator and perpetrator's family are demonized, so much so that if family members of the perpetrator are murdered they are not even counted as victims; and (2) gun rights supporters refuse to allow anyone to discuss gun control in the wake of the shootings.

Diamond shows that at Red Lake the tribal community handled the tragedy much differently. Red Lake is an Ojibwe community. It is a closed reservation, which means in Minnesota it was the only

Ojibwe reservation not opened by the United States to non-Indian settlement. The origin story of the Red Lake Reservation is riddled with bad stuff and terrible actions but also with good stuff, such as the survival of Anishinaabe people, language, and culture. The Red Lake community's response to their terrible tragedy was about making adults and institutions accountable. That community was honest about its origin stories and about its own failures.

The Constitution's origin story derives from rebellion and freedom from oppression, yes, but also slavery and Indian-hating. The Supreme Court likes to emphasize the good stuff, but not the bad stuff. Not addressing the bad stuff is dishonest. That's where mindless, tone-deaf, and damaging decisions such as *Heller* come from.

Traditional Anishinaabe people take principles such as Mino-Bimaadiziwin seriously. Everything is connected. Perhaps the worst thing an Anishinaabe person can do is to seek personal revenge. Recall that part of the Anishinaabe origin story, which is really a story of apocalypse, beginning with an act of revenge. In a small, insular community where the margin of error between survival and starvation is tiny, the loss of any individual person is devastating. A crime that ends one Anishinaabe life is nearly catastrophic. A return crime of revenge makes matters doubly, triply worse. The Anishinaabeg were nearly ended by revenge killings in their origin stories; revenge is an existential threat. Entire tribal communities can be undone by revenge and, more generally, violence. This is an ancient lesson learned by the Anishinaabeg at an early time and, hopefully, remains a foundational teaching. It is a teaching of peace and respect. It serves as a source of the Anishinaabe theory of Mino-Bimaadiziwin and the Seven Grandfathers (or Grandmothers). It is a story of honesty, too, of acknowledgment of error.

Americans made terrible errors in ratifying their Constitution. Portions of those errors have been undone by amendments to the Constitution – the ban on slavery, equal protection, voting rights expansions – but bigoted relics such as the right to bear arms remain. It's long past time for the United States to address its own origin story.

2

LEWIS CASS AND THE ANISHINAABE ALLIES OF THE BRITISH

The western Great Lakes Anishinaabeg used to tell the story of Snapping Turtle.[39] Snapping Turtle was always rallying for war. For his first war, he conscripted his own sons to form an army of snapping turtles. They fought a legendary battle, with terrific magic and heroism, but in the end all of Snapping Turtle's sons were killed. Snapping Turtle himself was captured and held prisoner for years. He eventually used trickery to escape. But he tried to raise another army to lead into war and glory. At first, no one would join Snapping Turtle the second time. He was a failed military leader, and he seemed to be rallying for a pointless war. But then the Painted Turtles stood up and said they would join him. Snapping Turtle asked them what they would do in a fight, and they showed him by immediately retreating into their shells. Snapping Turtle shook his head, but no one else was stepping up to follow him, so he said it was good enough and went to war. The rest writes itself, with the twist that the people of the second town that Snapping Turtle attacked were delighted to make an enormous pot of soup out of his Painted Turtle allies.

In the esteemed pages of the *North American Review*,[40] the American ambassador to France, Lewis Cass, bitterly condemned the hated British in 1840 for giving presents to Michigan Indians on Drummond Island, Manitoulin Island, and elsewhere on the borderlands between the United States and Canada. Cass had once been the territorial governor of Michigan, the superintendent of Indian affairs before statehood, and then secretary of war under Andrew Jackson. When the *Review* originally published Cass's 1840 article, he was ambassador to France. When the *Review* reprinted the article, the editors knew more about Cass's legacy and felt obliged to mention that Cass really despised the British.

Cass hated Indians, too, perhaps most especially the Michigan Indians who met with the British in the 1830s and 1840s. Cass was Andrew Jackson's ally, and did much of the dirty work politically and on the ground to remove Indian people from the eastern lands to lands west of the Mississippi.[41] Cass at times might have deployed the rhetoric used by Jackson's people that Indian people were doomed unless they became physically separated from Americans and ultimately gave in to civilization – that all looked good in the press and salved the concerns of the nineteenth-century snowflakes, but Indians were his geopolitical enemy.

Keep in mind that as secretary of war, Cass supervised Michigan Indian agent Henry Schoolcraft in the 1836 treaty negotiations with the Michigan Ottawa Indian nations.[42] Cass and Schoolcraft, with the help of a handful of fur traders who stood to gain from treaty-related payouts, led three dozen *ogimaag* (leaders) to Washington, D.C., where they apparently met Andrew Jackson at a reception or some other function. Jackson told Cass to instruct Schoolcraft to negotiate a removal treaty, one in which the Michigan Ottawas agreed to remove to Iowa or Kansas or some such place. The lower-peninsula Anishinaabe treaty delegation selected Aishquagonabe from Grand Traverse to serve as the speaker.[43]

The treaty did not turn out as the Anishinaabeg thought it would, allowing the cession of what would quickly become about one-third of the land mass of the new state of Michigan in 1837. But neither did it turn out very well for Lewis Cass's demand for removal. The 1836 treaty tribes are still there. Five are federally recognized nations – Grand Traverse Band of Ottawa and Chippewa Indians, Little Traverse Bay Bands of Odawa Indians, Little River Band of Ottawa Indians, Bay Mills Indian Community, and Sault Ste. Marie Tribe of Chippewa Indians. Others, like the Burt Lake Band of Ottawa Indians and the Grand River Band of Ottawa Indians, stand a fair chance of federal recognition in the coming years.

In the years following the 1836 treaty, many Anishinaabeg moved away, usually to stay with relations in Ontario, Canada, which is also part of Anishinaabewaki (the traditional territory of the Anishinaabeg). Some Indians did their due diligence and visited those proposed western lands in Iowa and Kansas, but they were not interested. Anishinaabewaki is woodlands country, with trees and water aplenty. The plains are missing trees and, too often, water. The game and fowl are different, there is no maple sugar bush or wild rice, and there are no ceremonial places familiar to the Anishinaabe. Plus, the area was home to other Indian nations, both Indigenous and others whom the United States had removed. Most importantly, Anishinaabewaki is where the ancestors are buried, and to leave that place was like certain death, as Aishquagonabe and his nephew, Aghosa, once stated.[44] The Michigan Indians that did remain negotiated a rather heroic effort to adapt and maintain.

One of those adaptation strategies, championed by *ogimaag* like Aishquagonabe and Assiginack, was to meet annually with British Canada to receive presents (Assiginack and his family eventually left to live in Canada). Receiving presents was a thing, a strategy employed by the British for a century or more to maintain good relations with Indian tribes. It was a diplomatic feast hosted by the British, and Indians who came were supposed to be favored by the British for the coming year. And Indians got more than a feast – they returned home with trading goods.

Northern Michigan in the 1830s and 1840s was largely unsettled. Travel by canoe on the western Great Lakes waterway and plentiful inland waterways was fast and easy. The Americans had a presence on paper, but the Anishinaabeg were the most powerful entity in the area. And for the most part, they favored the British. Not only did the British give presents and engage with the Anishinaabeg in formal foreign relations, they knew better than to try to displace or remove Indian people. The Americans, on the other hand, wanted it all.

And Lewis Cass was the mouthpiece for Indian removal and American domination. His *North American Review* piece in 1840 presented an argument for readers that suggested the real problem was

British Canada. But likely Cass knew the real problem was Indians. The British would have little or no ability to interfere in American interests except that they had cultivated decent relations with Michigan Indians. In Cass's syllogistic worldview, that meant the Indians had to go. The real problem was Indians, Indians who were not and never would be American.

The 1840 piece was the fourth and final article Lewis Cass published on Indian affairs in the *North American Review*. The powerful and monstrous drive to remove Indian people from the East had largely succeeded. The United States succeeded, at horrific cost to Indian people, to force the bulk of the Cherokee, Choctaw, Creek, Chickasaw, and Seminole nations to Oklahoma. The federal government also succeeded in forcing out large portions of the Haudenosaunee nations in New York, ultimately to Wisconsin and Oklahoma. The Americans also forced most Ohio River valley tribes and southern Great Lakes tribes west.

But Lewis Cass had failed his Indian-hating president in not forcing the northern Michigan Anishinaabeg west, like the Seminole Indians who had escaped to the swamplands of Florida while harboring escaped slaves. It must have grated on Cass, the former Michigan territorial governor, who wrote in 1840 that the British and their Michigan Indian allies kept up their relations long after the Anishinaabeg supposedly submitted to the protection of the United States in the 1836 treaty. History shows those Indian–British relationships never grew into a serious threat to American interests, instead remaining relatively minor irritants. But at the time, Cass wanted the Anishinaabeg out of northern Michigan and the British punished for meddling. He never got what he wanted, which of course was war. War would have been horrific for both sides in the northern Michigan summer, where mosquitoes and black flies would have devastated American armies, and in the winter, where fighters and families would have starved and frozen to death. Cass's hatred may have blinded him to these realities. Or maybe it was what he wanted all along. American leaders and their moneyed constituents love a good war.

Snapping Turtle was a warmonger, like Lewis Cass. And like Lewis Cass, Snapping Turtle was able to avoid the fate of his warriors and soldiers. In an alternative version of the story, Snapping Turtle called for warriors.[45] First, the Moose nation appeared and asked to join the war party. Snapping Turtle rejected the Moose nation because its legs were vulnerable to attack by missile. Next, the Bear nation appeared and asked to join the war party. Again, Snapping Turtle rejected the Bear nation because he concluded that bear legs were also vulnerable to attack by missile. Snapping Turtle accepted the painted turtles because their legs could be retracted and were not vulnerable to attack by missile. But in this version of the story, the same fate befell the poor painted turtles, who were turned into a massive pot of soup. But pernicious Snapping Turtle survived, became a hero, and had other adventures.

3

THE OSAGE NATION'S TRUSTEE

The famed Anishinaabe trickster god, Nanaboozhoo, was out hunting one day.[46] Nanaboozhoo had no relatives, no parents, no one to teach him the skills he needed to survive in Anishinaabewaki (the world of the Anishinaabeg). He was also a bad listener, and did things his own way. So he hunted alone, which meant he really could only hunt smaller creatures such as beaver and muskrat. Larger animals like deer and moose required multiple hunters. Nanaboozhoo was always looking for an edge, and one day he discovered the skunk. He saw the skunk shoot a stream of liquid that stank horribly and that drove off a large dog who wanted to eat the skunk. Nanaboozhoo wanted that power. He believed he could use it to hunt the larger creatures and also get revenge on enemies that had humiliated him in the past. He sought and found the skunk. He asked the skunk for the skunk's power. The skunk warned Nanaboozhoo that the foul odor that kept away predators and enemies also kept away friends and neighbors. There also was only a limited amount of stench power. It wasn't unlimited. Nanaboozhoo didn't care. He used his shapeshifting powers to turn himself into a skunk. Almost immediately, all the forest creatures mocked him and ran away when they saw him. Nanaboozhoo was fine with that for a time, but eventually he lost his temper and sprayed a group of raccoons that were mocking him. The stench was horrible, and the animals ran off screaming and the plants around him withered and died. Even Nanaboozhoo passed out from the smell. When he awoke, he wandered off until he found some deer. He tried his skunk powers again, but he had wasted his odor retaliating against the raccoons. When he pointed his rump at the deer and squeezed, all that came out was a fart.

For the Anishinaabe, waste was anathema.

In Anishinaabe communities throughout known history, Indian people rarely were wealthy. In winter and spring, when food stores were low, every piece of dried fruit, vegetable, and meat mattered. Every Indian person had to hunt, fish, farm, and gather for their daily subsistence all year-round. Every arrow, every bullet, every trap, every seed, every coat, every blanket mattered. Anishinaabe *ogimaag* (leaders) often were the people best at generating resources and so could share with others. Sharing was leadership. Sharing was power.

Nanaboozhoo's skunk story was a tale of selfishness and waste. He had one chance to take down a deer or other large creature, but instead he wasted his power on punishing raccoons for laughing at him. Nanaboozhoo was a supernatural creature with extraordinary power, but he was no leader. He didn't possess any influence over people. He was a joke. But he was still Anishinaabe.

In the early twentieth century, many of the people of the Osage Nation found themselves wealthy.[47] The United States confined the Osages, who originally called Missouri, northern Arkansas, eastern Kansas, and parts of Oklahoma their homelands, in northeastern Oklahoma. The land wasn't any good for farming, which is very much what the federal government wanted the Osages to do; it was, however, located on top of massive oil pockets. Congress severed the subsurface property interest from the surface lands and placed ownership in the federal government, to be held in trust for the Osages. The Department of the Interior would manage the oil interests for them, negotiating all the oil leases with powerful oil barons, collecting royalties, and paying the proceeds to the Osages.

Before long, Osages were wealthy. They were buying cars. They were buying houses. They were sending their kids to prominent boarding schools. They were vacationing in Europe. Americans came to view the Osages as the wealthiest people in the world. And Americans quickly grew jealous and angry over the Osage wealth, these savages who came into money by mere accident. Local and national newspapers drilled racist stereotypes into the American readers about the ridiculous, idiot Indians who were wasting their cash on junk and getting robbed.

THE OSAGE NATION'S TRUSTEE

If nothing else, members of Congress then and now can see easy political points when shoved in their faces. Something would have to be done about these Indians, newspaper commentators were saying. So Congress held hearings. The Department of the Interior had sent an investigator to examine the finances of the wealthy Osage full-blood Indians. His name was H. S. Traylor, and he hated Indian people.

The government had already sent Traylor the investigator into the breach before. In 1916, Traylor reported back from the Navajo Reservation that Navajo people were encroaching and that the reservation should be partitioned to benefit Hopi people. He blamed the Hopi people for their troubles, calling "the Hopi . . . the most pitiable and contemptible coward who now lives upon the face of the earth. . . . Were he otherwise than the coward that he is, he would prefer to die fighting rather than to surrender the resources of his territory to an enemy."[48] In 1917, the commissioner of Indian Affairs sent Traylor to northern Wisconsin to investigate claims by Anishinaabe people that the allotments they had selected were too swampy, and that they wanted to select different allotments. He studied the claims and recommended the rejection of most, but not all. He blamed an *ogema* (leader) named Kah-quo-dos for agitating for a conspiracy to complain about the allotments. Traylor hated Kah-quo-dos:

> This man is absolutely devoid of character and principle and is in no way worthy of the least recognition from the department. In his 52 years of life he has never worked, but has been a grafter and moocher upon the resources of his neighbors and friends. He is by far the hardest drinker among the Potawatomies and seldom draws a sober breath when he has the money and opportunity to secure whisky. Practically every word he speaks and every action he has prove him a liar and a man devoid of all good characteristics.[49]

Traylor was a judgmental investigator, to say the least. The Osages were in for a treat.

The commissioner then sent Traylor to Osage County in early 1918 "to obtain . . . first-hand information concerning the expenditure of large amounts of money by these Indians, and to investigate the wasteful and extravagant manner of the full bloods, and to furnish . . . such data as are necessary to present certain proposed legislation to Congress for the restriction of their moneys."[50] Traylor's job was to locate facts to justify a recommendation by the Department of the Interior to Congress to strip the Osages of the right to spend their own money. Traylor's report speaks for itself:

> When my work tends to the improvement and betterment of the Indians, I enter upon it with at least some degree of avidity, eagerness, and hope of success, but such inspiration is always lacking when I enter the Osage Nation. The experiences had, the observations made, the facts established, the sins boldly flaunted, vices openly displayed, revolt the soul and sicken the heart of anyone who has been taught that temperance in all things, simplicity in living, truth in every word, and character in all dealings are necessary to a true citizenship and to a fairly perfect civic state.
>
> The devil was certainly in control on that day when agreements and ratifications were made between the Osage people, the department, and Congress, and his majesty has certainly been in high glee at the subsequent results and the marked accomplishments. I have visited and worked in and about most of the cities of our country, and am more or less familiar with their filthy sores and iniquitous cesspools, yet I never wholly appreciated the story of Sodom and Gomorrah, whose sins and vices proved their undoing and their downfall, until I visited this Indian nation. . . No doubt is in my mind that were a destroying angel, with a like humane and forgiving heart, as had the one thousands of years ago, hovering over Osage, he could not find the necessary deserving ones to save their country from the penalty visited upon those of Biblical history who had forgotten the laws of their God.[51]

The government inspector's conclusion was that there were not enough good Osages around to justify not divinely eradicating the whole of the Osage Nation off the face of the earth and sending them down to his idea of hell:

> There are, of course, some in the Osage Nation who live in virtue and in obedience to divine and statutory law. There are certainly some who live in denial and economy. There are surely some who possess the spirit and character of true men and women, but the one who comes occasionally on an official mission must see only the thousands of harpies sitting upon every promonotory [*sic*] vomiting their filth, disease, and pestilence upon those who pass beneath. The present counterpart of that mythical vulture has not deteriorated, but has grown in strength and success. He yet strikes his prey with a full power and they sicken and die. All the forces of dissipation and evil are here found. Gambling, drinking, adultery, lying, thieving, murdering prevail and have their hourly victims.[52]

Ironic that Traylor blamed the Osages themselves for the murders that were just beginning when he visited Osage County. His informants likely knew about the grand conspiracy that was in play to kill Osage people for their wealth. He asked the non-Osages of Osage County their impressions of the Osage people, now that they had riches. His informants were not impressed with the Osages:

> I am requested to report what disposition is being made of these moneys by the full-blood Indians. An accurate and truthful answer could be given you in a few words, "that all of it is being spent and wasted." . . . Every white man in Osage County will tell you that the Indians are now running wild, not only spending their incomes in full, but going hundreds of thousands of dollars in debt each year.[53]

Traylor concluded that even the Indians who could be "considered one of the best Indians on the reservation" were wastrels, buying expensive cars and hiring other people ("Negroes") to do their work on their farms. Traylor listed several of the Osages he considered "wild ones" and accused them of purchasing way too many cars, drinking too much, and going into debt. Traylor's informants, of course, were the group of people that stood to gain access to Osage wealth if Congress denied the Osages of their legal competency by becoming their guardians. But that's what Traylor was supposed to do, draw broad, negative generalizations about Osage people to justify denying them their property rights:

> The above dissipations are typical to all of the Osages. While one or two of them show an exceptional expenditure for cars, yet all of the Osage full bloods spend money in like amounts and for like purposes. They seemingly know no restraint, and will buy and borrow anything and any amount which the merchants and bankers will intrust [sic] them.[54]

Traylor also described how Osage households hired others, poor brown and white people he called "pot lickers," to perform their farming and household chores for them, work that Traylor was quick to note would be done without resorting to hired help by "a white farmer and his family":

> When I began to visit the Indian homes and allotments I discovered in part, at least, a cause for such great expenditures. Each one was surrounded by "pot lickers," as they are known in this section. These are Negroes, Mexicans, and white trash who surround each Indian family, and who do a minimum amount of work for a maximum wage. The Osage Indian and his family simply will not turn a hand to do the least thing. They will not feed horses, draw water, clean barns, mend fences, dig cellars, paint houses, or any of that necessary and incessant work which forever continues about and around a successful

farm. I saw at one place no less than half a dozen of these people and in some instances a score or more. I saw at one place seven strong, able-bodied men digging a small cellar and placing a new fence around the house, all of which work would have been done by a white farmer and his family. These seven men during my few minutes' visit were not accomplishing what should have been done by any two of them in the same time. The Indians testify that they pay the heads of these families $30, $40, and $50 per month, and furnish them with quarters, fuel, and sustenance. All the laborers live well and draw from the Indians an immense amount of groceries.[55]

Traylor relied on the records of the non-Osage shop owners that sold these "groceries" to Osage people. He also detailed Osage car purchases and maintenance expenses. He was unhappy with local garage owners who seemed happy to overcharge Osage people for their car maintenance, but he was disgusted with how the Osages bought cars, ruined them quickly, and then bought even more expensive cars:

The Osage Indian will do absolutely nothing to his own car, but at the least defect runs it into a machine shop for repair. Each garage man is quite sure that every other garage man than himself robs them outrageously on all repair work. Several told me that the Indian would not even repair a puncture to a tire, but would continue his run into town at full speed, therewith destroying often a new and costly casing. Many times in their reckless driving they bend a fender, destroy a wheel, or break a top, and then they take that practically new car and trade it to some auto dealer for a grand new one, receiving as a compensation for the old hardly one-third of its value. Indians have been known to thus trade their cars because they were covered with mud. At best the car will not survive the fearful driving and absolute lack of attention given them longer than a few months. The young Indians are now becoming dissatisfied with the standard make of

cars at reasonable prices, and are beginning to purchase
Marmons, Stutz, Premiers, and other expensive makes.[56]

These are not comments from a man who worried for the Osages
that they were not being careful with their newfound wealth. These
are not comments from a man who hoped the best for these Indians,
people who only a few decades before had their homes stripped from
them by the United States. Indian people are not unique in having dif-
ficulty managing wealth. Sadly, it is natural for people to glom onto
wealthier people and try to extract some of that wealth for themselves.
It seems likely that Osage County businesspeople were taking advantage of the newly rich Osages. Given that the United States owes a
duty of protection to Indians all over, a federal government investigation of that situation seems rational. But H. S. Traylor's investigation
was a complete travesty. He drew every possible conclusion that the
Osage people were hopelessly evil and deranged. He gave the commissioner of Indian Affairs what he wanted, a report demanding that
Congress strip the Osages of their property. Congress eventually did
enact a law that continued the guardianship laws in place that dominated the Osages of Osage County. In 1921, Congress reaffirmed the
Osages legally incompetent, unless they were mixed blood. Perhaps
Traylor's report contributed to the political will necessary to enact
such onerous, even fascistic, laws on the Osage people.

The horrific coda to this story dwarfs the near-comical Indian-hating of the government inspector. Although the oil business was managed in trust by the United States, the federal government treated the
arrangement as a guardianship. Full-blood Osages were "incompetent," effectively children under the law, who could not be trusted to
take care of themselves. "Incompetents" need guardians to manage
their wealth for them. The federal government handed over Osage
trust assets to wealthy and powerful whites in Osage County, who
outrageously and corruptly mismanaged those assets – perhaps that
same people who talked to Traylor. Worse, Osage full-blood women
who married "competent" men (almost always white men) effectively
married their guardian. In literally dozens of instances, and perhaps
hundreds (no one knows for sure), these guardians murdered their

wards, who were also their wives, in order to secure the Osage trust asset. Dozens. Perhaps hundreds. But that's another story.

The Americans asserting control over Indian resources and assets demanded a form of frugality that to Indian people was like hoarding. American trustees and guardians, and I use those terms ironically, insisted the Osage people not spend their money freely but rather spend it on items and services acceptable to trustees and guardians. But that's not really why the people dominating Osage lives wanted frugality. They too often had self-interest in mind and controlled Osage assets for their own benefit under a veneer of fiduciary responsibility.

Anishinaabe people considered waste and excess to be inconsistent with Mino-Bimaadiziwin. This principle favoring frugality and humility appears to have been rooted in the practicality of living in a world of great turmoil and upheaval when non-Anishinaabe people began to invade Anishinaabewaki. Wealth, when acquired, was to be shared. Other Indian people, including the Osage people, likely preached the same principle of generosity, like the skunk in the Nanaboozhoo story.

Nanaboozhoo's hilarious skunk-odor story was a warning to Anishinaabe people. People without ethics might come to Indian people pretending to advise responsibility, but instead act with a bad purpose. Nanaboozhoo paid a price of sorts when he used up his skunk spray for spurious reasons, but said Indian people too often have paid a terrific price when Americans wasted – and stole – Indian resources.

THE EXPERIMENT OF ASSIMILATION

Two young Anishinaabe *ininiwaag* (men) fasted in advance of setting out to learn the source of thunder in the clouds.[57] They fasted for eight days before setting out on their journey. Then they headed toward a mountain covered in clouds. The sounds of thunder became louder as they got closer. They climbed the mountain. As they went closer to the summit, the clouds parted. The Anishinaabe *ininiwaag* then saw the source of the thunder: two enormous birds with two chicks. Each time the birds opened their eyes, lightning flashed. Each time the birds opened their beaks, thunder sounded. One of the Anishinaabe youths wanted a closer look. The other stayed behind. The curious and more adventurous youth moved closer. Suddenly, the Thunderbirds (Animikii Binesiwaag) looked directly at the youth. They struck him with lightning and killed him instantaneously. The other youth ran off. Anishinaabe people have stayed away from the mountain ever since.

This story contains many themes. The Anishinaabe *ininiwaag* properly prepared for an important journey – a journey of discovery, a journey of inherent danger. They fasted for eight days. In many Anishinaabe stories, fasting is critically important in preparing for a journey. The longer the fast, the stronger the Anishinaabe, the better the journey. Eight days is a very long time to fast, normally meaning the journey will be very successful. And for the most part, the journey of these two Anishinaabe *ininiwaag* was very successful. They climbed a mountain, a mountain covered in clouds. They did so in the face of tremendous thunder and lightning. They climbed high enough to pass through the clouds. They reached a vantage point whereby they witnessed the powerful *animikiiwaag* (Thunderbirds) at the summit of this mountain. It goes wrong there. One Anishinaabe <u>*inini*</u> is too curious, too adventurous. This *inini* is not judicious in his curiosity, in his journey of discovery. He is too experimental, too arrogant. He is not respectful of the ways of the *animikiiwaag*, these Thunderbirds. He thinks he knows better. It goes terribly wrong. He is killed.

The story of the two Anishinaabe *ininiwaag* and the Animikii Binesiwaag is an example of the meaning and workings of some of the Seven Grandfather (or Grandmother) teachings, namely courage, wisdom, humility, love, and respect. The Anishinaabe *ininiwaag* showed great courage and wisdom in their preparations for their journey and in the journey itself. They showed respect in fasting, anticipating the deeply spiritual character of the upcoming journey. Their journey was indeed arduous, and they showed great courage in climbing the mountain into the unknown. The young man who held back showed great wisdom and humility – wisdom to know that the Thunderbird adults would be extremely protective of their brood, humble enough to keep his distance, to know the power of the love of a family. The youth who ventured forth did not follow these teachings.

Nineteenth-century federal Indian policy too often was an uncontrolled experiment. American policy makers were never quite sure what to do with Indian people and tribal nations. The first policy makers, the Founders, were not even consistent on what their goals were in relation to Indian affairs, with one exception – they wanted Indians gone. How to get rid of Indians, what to do once Indians were gotten rid of, and what to do when Indians couldn't be gotten rid of was then, and still is, a prime source of conflict and confusion.

Early on, most American policy makers realized that merely sending in the military to drive Indians out was not viable. In 1785, the United States invaded Indian country in the Ohio River Valley.[58] The American military force sent in first was completely destroyed. So was the second, and the third. That war, sometimes known as the Northwest Indian War, took ten years for the Americans to prosecute.

The costs were tremendous. So sending in the army in every situation wasn't viable.

The Americans realized that killing all the Indians was inefficient, so the federal government tried other strategies. Trade. Alliance building. Deceit. Coercion. Disease. Bounties. Even so, despite its defeats, the government tried war again and again when other strategies failed. Anything that worked. No moral boundaries existed. Indians were, after all, barely human, savages, incompetent. By the late nineteenth century, commentators declared the American frontier "closed." But there were still millions of acres of land owned or occupied by Indians peppering the American Midwest and West. Americans had been experimenting with what to do with Indians who could not be gotten rid of for centuries. By the mid- to late-nineteenth century, the federal government turned its Indian affairs political capital to experiments in assimilating these remaining Indians.

Missing in the development of these social experiments were forethought and consideration. Instead, the plans and their implementation were riddled with ethnocentrism and Indian-hating. Consider the 1846 report of the commissioner of Indian affairs, William Medill.[59] A former congressman from Ohio, Medill knew little about Indian people. Before President James Polk appointed him commissioner, he was the number-three official under the postmaster general, so what he "knew" about Indian people was virtually nothing. And yet he was the federal government's lead official in the field. The report began with what Medill "knew" about "red m[e]n," or what he called "an interesting people, who once held undisputed sway over the territory we now occupy, but who have gradually melted away before the advance of civilization, or, in broken groups, been swept westward by the pressure and rapid extension of a more intelligent and enterprising race."[60] This was Indian-hating clumsily disguised as respect and sympathy. Commissioner Medill condemned Indians with faint praise as "interesting," past their prime as a people. Meanwhile, he implied that Indian people are unintelligent, uncivilized, and lazy. This was a sloppy and careless piece of professional work that would not stand even the slimmest of scrutiny now, but his audience of nineteenth-century American men, white men in power in the Department of War and in Congress, likely already accepted these precepts. And it likely was all they "knew" about Indian people.

The report was also a defense. Medill acknowledged that terrible things had happened to Indian people as a result of American action, but that injury was mere collateral damage, justifiable. He wrote, "While, to all, the fate of the red man has, thus far, been alike unsatisfactory and painful, it has, with many, been a source of much misrepresentation and unjust national reproach."[61] Criticism of Indian affairs, he argued, was unjustified because, after all, "apathy, barbarism, and heathenism must give way to energy, civilization, and christianity."[62] The Indians to whom Medill served as protector, guardian, and trustee were, to him, lazy, savage, and pagan. Injuries to people like that really could not be so bad, Medill argued. The leader of the federal government's Indian affairs administration also blamed lazy and apathetic Indians themselves for not doing enough to stop the dispossession of their lands and resources, their lives and culture. The commissioner assumed inherent savagery and barbarism in Indian cultures, which he essentially argued was a justification for the terrible things that had befallen Indian people at the hands of Americans and their government. Finally, Medill assumed Indian religious beliefs that deviate from Christianity further justified the bad things that happened to them. Medill's Indian-hating was as comprehensive as it was bland and simplistic.

Medill summarized the experimental federal Indian policy already tried by the United States. He mentioned the policy of "coloniz[ing] our Indian tribes beyond the reach, for some years, of our white population."[63] This sounds like Indian removal, a federal policy of confiscating Indian lands in the region east of the Mississippi River and forcing Indians on death marches toward the West. It was also a disturbing statement about what colonization meant to American policy makers, suggesting that any time one nation moved into a foreign land base, they were merely colonizing that new territory. As American history shows, too often the United States forced one tribal nation onto the lands of other tribal nations.

Medill then mentioned the policy of "confining each [tribal nation] within a small district of country, so that, as the game decreases and becomes scarce, the adults will gradually be compelled to resort to agriculture and other kinds of labor to obtain a subsistence."[64] This policy sounds like the reservation system. It was a candid admission that federal officials considered reservations, designed to "contain" Indian people, as what we might now call concentration camps. It also includes an ignorant assumption too often made by Americans about Indians, that they did not engage in agriculture. This assumption was patently false. Indians east of the Mississippi River in flood plains and other areas suitable for farming managed vast farms before their dispossession by colonists. For example, the Cherokee Nation famously exported corn to the undernourished citizens of the state of Georgia. There are drawings of the massive Three Sisters (corn, beans, and squash) farms managed by the Anishinaabe people of the Grand River valley in Michigan. The reservation system, however, too often moved Indian people to locations that were completely unsuitable for farming. Medill's invocation of the "scarcity" of game would hardly be taken as a good public policy choice now, given that Indian people forced to live on lands unsuitable for farming who could also not hunt for subsistence had to resort to wage slavery with white employers in order to scratch out a feeble existence. Medill applauded this policy outcome, arguing that finally Indian people would go to work.

Medill added that the government had established "manual labor schools."[65] The government designed these schools to teach basic "letters" to Indian children.[66] For the boys, government schools taught agricultural and mechanical skills. For the girls, the schools taught skills in the various "branches of housewifery."[67] The government also introduced Christian missionaries to Indian people. Mandatory boarding schools would come to dominate in the decades that followed.[68] Medill condemned Indian men for other stereotypes, namely that Indian men were predisposed to war and treated work with disdain, leaving Indian women to suffer with all the labor. Men like Medill gave up on Indian adults. Instead, Americans like Medill believed schooling Indian children in American ways would change the culture of Indian communities. This was nothing new. Ivy League schools such as Dartmouth and Harvard were founded to educate Indian children in this way long before the American Republic was founded.[69]

Americans were always experimenting with Indian people, attempting to change Indian cultures, attempting to make Indians assimilate or die, but not really caring which. Federal Indian policy was driven exclusively by American political and economic interests. On rare occasions, policy makers like Medill might have acknowledged the harsh consequences of federal policy on Indian people. But also like Medill, they would have couched those apologies with apologist Indian-hating statements blaming Indians themselves for their dire circumstances.

Some might disagree with the characterization of these federal policies as evidence of the disrespect Americans showed Indian people. But compare assimilationist policy with modern-day self-determination policy, which features federal funding of tribally controlled government services. For example, instead of using federal government–mandated educational curricula, modern tribes can accept federal funding to establish their own schools. Some tribes have even started successful Indigenous language immersion programs.

Anishinaabe tribal governments experiment, too, but when they are planning for their own children, their own futures, they do so with a great emphasis on the Seven Grandfathers (or Grandmothers). Other tribes do the same with their own cultural precepts.

Love. Wisdom. Humility. Respect. Truth. Honesty. Courage.

These are the characteristics the Animikii Binesiwaag expected from Anishinaabe people and their leaders. But it's also what Indian people expect from their governments. Indian tribes too often have insufficient funding for adequate schools, health care, law enforcement, and so on, because they lack an adequate tax base, and they lack an adequate tax base because of federal policies like allotment. Nearly all the government revenue Indian tribes generate goes back to tribal members as services. Imagine what they could do with more.

5

ALLOTMENT — THIS IS NOT YOUR WAY TO GET FOOD

Nanaboozhoo used to travel all around, visiting his Anishinaabe relatives and the creatures of Anishinaabewaki (the world of the Anishinaabe).[70] One morning, he came to the house of Andahaunahquodishkung, the moose. The house was bountiful. Inside lived Andahaunahquodishkung's wife and seven children, a Mishomis (grandfather), and other people. Nanaboozhoo visited for a time and the noon hour approached. No one was preparing a noon meal, and he was getting hungry, and a little worried. In fact, Nanaboozhoo could see no food or supplies at all in the home. Then, right before noon, Andahaunahquodishkung's wife stood and put a kettle of water on the fire. Nanaboozhoo relaxed but still could see no actual food. Suddenly, Andahaunahquodishkung stood, grabbed a sharp knife, walked over to his wife, lifted her shirt, and carved a piece of flesh from her back. Nanaboozhoo watched, shocked, as the wife took the flesh and prepared an entire meal from her own flesh. Her wounds healed quickly. The meal was delicious. "What an easy way to get food," Nanaboozhoo thought. "I won't have to hunt anymore."

Afterward, Nanaboozhoo invited Andahaunahquodishkung and his entire family over for lunch the next day. They gratefully accepted. When they arrived for lunch, Nanaboozhoo's wife said to him, "But we have nothing to cook for your guests." Nanaboozhoo shook his head gently, and told her not to worry. As the noon hour approached, he grabbed a knife and walked over to his wife. He lifted her shirt and carved out a piece of her flesh.

She screamed in pain and began bleeding profusely. Andahaunahquod-ishkung quickly jumped up and held his hand over her wound, sealing it and then healing it. He took the knife, carved flesh from his own body, and the group used his flesh to cook and eat a delicious lunch. After the meal, Andahaunahquodishkung said to Nanaboozhoo, "It is not in your nature to get food this way." Nanaboozhoo sagely nodded in agreement.

The Anishinaabe who lived around the southern end of Lake Michigan farmed enormous fields of corn, beans, and squash, the fabled Three Sisters. Certain strains of these plants grow together almost perfectly. The resulting mass of plant life seems messy and confused, but these plants nourish and fertilize each other, and even collectively serve to create natural pest repellents. The Three Sisters are like a microcosm of Mino-Bimaadiziwin. The Anishinaabe people lived seasonally, moving from the farmlands in the summer to the winter lodges farther inland into the forests where there would be some shelter from the harsh weather. In the spring, they would move again to the swampy areas to harvest the sugar bush. There was a harmony and a structure to all of this.

The coming of the French and then the British disrupted this lifeway, but the Anishinaabe adapted. They intermarried with the French and British, and as Lewis Cass complained,[71] even allied themselves with the British. But the Americans undid everything. They disrupted, then destroyed. First, the Americans took the southern farmlands in treaties that were at least partly negotiated in fraud, coercion, and bad faith. The Americans forced many southern Lake Michigan Indians to the west, away from their waters and their forests, where the Three Sisters did not thrive. The Americans moved the southern Lake Michigan Anishinaabeg again and again, to Kansas and Oklahoma. None of those places allowed the Anishinaabeg to thrive. They are prairie lands prone to drought, lacking natural defensive infrastructure from other Indian nations and hostile white people.

Worse, even when the Anishinaabe nations could establish a permanent home on a reservation, the Americans still did not stop. They tore up the treaty provisions establishing these permanent homes and carved them up into allotments. George Manypenny, the commissioner of Indian Affairs in the mid-nineteenth century, insisted upon allotment provisions in the treaties he negotiated with several Midwest and Great Plains Indian tribes.

Allotment is a dirty word for most American Indians. The process, in a nutshell, is this.[72] Take an Indian reservation owned collectively by a tribal nation. Subdivide the reservation into 40-, 80-, and 160-acre parcels, regardless of prior reservation land use practices. Force tribal citizens, usually male heads of household, to select a parcel. Whatever land was left over, the government put up for sale on the public market. Give that person – now known as an allottee – a certificate describing the parcel and also stating the parcel is to be held by the federal government in trust for twenty-five years. During that time, the allotment parcel will not be taxable by local governments (reservation land is not taxable by state and local governments, by the way, unless Congress says so). The theory of the Americans who thought up this process was that Indians would delight in finally being the owners of individual parcels of land. And some Indians did. In this theory, Indian landowners would learn to exploit and improve the land, to become farmers like so many other Americans. Most of the time, the federal government divided up the reservation in a way that forced selection from the least valuable reservation land. And at the end of the twenty-five-year trust period, Indians were no more likely to be farmers than before. Many times, Indian allottees never even moved to their allotment. But the land became taxable, and so suddenly Indians had tax bills to deal with. Tax liens followed, then foreclosures. Soon state and local governments – and many non-Indians – owned many of the Indian allotments. What once had been a reservation collectively owned by a tribal nation was carved up like a Thanksgiving turkey. Allotted reservations in the present day look like checkerboards of complicated jurisdiction and competing land uses. Kind of what a turkey looks like after everyone has eaten.

In his opening speech to the Lake Mohonk Conference of the Friends of the Indian in 1900, the chairman of the Board of Indian Commissioners, Merrill Gates, described allotment as a "mighty pulverizing engine for the breaking up the tribal mass."[73] Gates, newly elected to the presidency of that organization, opened his speech by reciting the purpose of the group, which was to best assimilate what he called the lesser races of the American empire – Indians, "Negro[s]," Filipinos, and so on – in other words, "people who are not fit for self-government."[74] For Indians, that meant changing federal Indian policy: "The old way dealt with Indians by tribes and in the mass; the new way deals with them as families and individuals."[75]

Gates applauded an 1871 act of Congress that stated the United States would no longer enter into new treaties with Indian tribes.[76] The law is most likely unconstitutional because it purports to bar the president and the Senate from negotiating, ratifying, and declaring treaties with Indian tribes in contravention of the US Constitution. Indian tribes probably hadn't even heard of the law for decades, in no small part because the federal government kept negotiating with Indian tribes, "ratifying" these agreements as legislation passed by both the House and the Senate. But never mind that. Gates praised the law because, in his view, it meant the end of Indian wars. No longer would Indian tribes, in his view, arrogantly take up arms against the United States, because only an actual nation can fight a war. The key for Gates was that the United States, on paper anyway, had begun to focus on dealing with the "Indian problem" as a problem of Indian "individuals," not Indian "nations."

Gates rudely claimed that tribal life was a life of "savagery."[77] Displaying breathless ethnocentrism, he argued that tribal customs forced Indian people into a form of "tyrann[ical,] . . . absolute conform[ity.]"[78] Gates argued that Indian people dedicated to the tribal community were denying themselves good old "Christian" and civilized American individualism. He asserted that Indian people just hadn't evolved into civilized people yet, unlike white Christian Americans. Religion and education, he argued, could perform the civilizing work of hundreds of thousands of years of biological evolution in one generation. He promised to dedicate his work with the Friends of the Indian to that end.

Gates lamented the history of federal Indian policy up to that point. He acknowledged that the Americans had treated Indian people to a "Century of Dishonor," borrowing the description Helen Hunt Jackson used as the title to her 1881 polemic tome.[79] One might think that Gates was about to acknowledge, as Helen Hunt Jackson did, that the government had betrayed Indian tribes and Indian people, killed them, starved them, exposed them to disease, robbed them of their lands and resources. Not Gates. Instead, he lamented that the Americans had not exposed Indian people to European culture much earlier and more forcefully. The "measured separatism," Charles Wilkinson's phrase,[80] of the treaty and reservation eras was a huge mistake, according to Chairman Gates. All it did was delay the evolution of Indian people into human beings. For Gates, the most critical impact of the reservation strategy was the creation of lawless nations within the United States. Quoting Hiram Price's 1884 report to Congress, Gates alleged, "The Indian was not answerable to any law for injuries committed on one of his own race in the Indian country; and the result is that the most brutal murders are committed and the murderer goes unwhipped of justice."[81] Ironic it is, the American civilization whipping criminals, literally or figuratively.

For Gates, allotment was the manifestation of a powerful strategy that would allow Indians to evolve into civilized beings. Gates believed allotment meant Indian allottees could acquire American citizenship. They would then be able to drop their allegiances to tribal nations and instead give their patriotism to the United States. He believed Indian people needed to abandon their tribal ways in order to become human. For Gates, American citizenship and loyalty to American states and territories meant Indians would turn away from their own cultures and traditions, which he harshly condemned: "Instead of a blind obedience to the dictates of deadening uniformity imposed by tribal life, those who accept the provisions of this law are summoned to a share in the varied interests and activities of civilization."[82]

Gates's condemnation of Indian culture as mindless conformity is the epitome of irony. Indian cultures were, and are, unusually opposed to conformity and uniformity. Traditional tribal leadership was not hierarchical, like American government. A tribal leader was not even first among equals. Tribal leaders were equals among equals. Nonconformity and opposition to the dictatorial orders from a leader who did nothing for the community to merit power were tenets of virtually all American Indian tribes. So many thousands of Indian people suffered horribly at the hands of Americans who demanded Indian

children live at religious or military boarding schools to rigidly conform.[83] Even now, many Indian people who are not churchgoers, for
example, find baffling the practices of Catholic and Protestant believers, singing and speaking in unison at the direction of a hierarchical
leadership embodied in a priest or preacher. Opposition to conformity
is the tool Indian people used to survive.

A hallmark of Indian culture is adaptability. A culture might iden-
tify a way of doing things, but when the circumstances change, the
culture must change, too. Michigan Anishinaabe people had been living under the regime of allotment since the 1850s,[84] and had nearly
a half century of experience with it before Merrill Gates acclaimed
its virtues. The Michigan Odawa people had negotiated for defined
and permanent reservations in 1836,[85] but those promises were unfulfilled. In the 1840s, because the federal government didn't survey
them properly or declare them reservations, Indians couldn't move
there legally. They managed to acquire land in fee through sympathetic white persons who were willing to act as shills for Indian pur-
chasers, but this land base was legally tenuous. Indians couldn't own
land under state law. So the tribes sought a new treaty and got one in
1855 that featured allotted reservations. Michigan Indians didn't really want allotment, but Commissioner George Manypenny thought
the same way Merrill Gates would decades later and insisted that
allotment be a part of the new Indian treaties his administration negotiated. The allotment plans were ridiculous disasters, with fraud,
incompetence, and corruption dominating the allotment process.
Some Indians did acquire allotments and manage to hold onto them,
including my own family, the Mamagonas in Antrim County, Michigan. Others were not so lucky, and became squatters on their own
lands. Land speculators illegally acquired the best lands for residen-
tial purposes and sold them at handsome profits to non-Indian people
– "summer" people. The large bulk of the remaining land went to
railroad and timber companies, which clear-cut all of northern Michigan's virgin timber, timber that today would likely be valued in the
billions of dollars. Michigan Anishinaabe scratched out a difficult
existence as their land base disappeared, their forests disappeared,
and their children were taken away to boarding schools en masse.
This was allotment in Michigan.

But somehow Indian people held on. Prior to allotment, Michigan Anishinaabe people lived seasonally. In the summers, they gravitated in large groups to the lakeshore, planting massive crops of the Three Sisters, hunting, fishing, and berry picking, storing food and supplies for a long winter. Some say the Lake Michigan shore from the Mackinac Straights to Waganakising, Little Traverse Bay, was a long metropolis of Anishinaabe villages and people. When winter came, Anishinaabe people relocated inland in smaller family units, sometimes moving only a few miles, but other times traveling all the way down to what is now Indiana and Illinois. As spring approached, Anishinaabe families reappeared in the inland sugar bush to harvest maple sugar. Then they moved to the shore again, repeating the cycle.

The promise of the reservations slowed and eventually halted that seasonal cycle of living. Allotment destroyed it completely. Within a few generations, Michigan Anishinaabe people were all but barred from rotating the locations of their homes. The forests that provided so much to the Anishinaabeg were gone. Access to the lakeshore was extremely limited. Indian adults turned to wage labor to make a living, a hard one at best. But they adapted and survived. By the mid-twentieth century, Michigan Anishinaabe people began to rediscover their fishing rights, eventually prevailing in court against the state of Michigan's efforts to stop them.[86]

Nanaboozhoo learned the hard way about the right way to get food. The story of his visit to the lodge of the moose, Andahaunahquodishkung, taught the Anishinaabeg that there is a right way and a wrong way to get food. Nanaboozhoo the trickster was sometimes the teacher and sometimes the student. In this story, he was the student. His folly in thinking he could take shortcuts taught two lessons. One lesson is that there are no shortcuts. The other is that the Anishinaabe people must seek to live in harmony with the earth. It's no mistake Andahaunahquodishkung is not human. He is a wild animal, a moose. A moose's obligations to the world, to earth, differ from the obligations of the Anishinaabeg. The Anishinaabeg should only accept what is offered by the earth, and then give thanks to the earth by offering semaa (tobacco), a sacred plant. The Anishinaabeg are not supposed to take from the earth, to make the earth into something unnatural. But allotment carved up the land, an effort to force the Anishinaabeg to control and dominate the earth. There are many reasons why that didn't and couldn't work.

And look what happened. Americans deforested all of Michigan. Michigan Anishinaabe people lost almost all their lands. Their governments went underground, meeting periodically in desperate efforts to respond to the federal government's policies.

But still the Anishinaabeg prevailed. They learned to depend more on fishing and hunting. They commodified their sugaring, canoe-building skills, and basketmaking skills. They adapted to the new wage-labor economy introduced by the Americans. They were the ones who introduced cherry and apple orchards that northern Michigan is known for now. And now that Michigan tribal governments are often the lead economic engines in their various regions; they are leading the way to protecting the earth, from which the food comes. Nanaboozhoo would be proud of his people.

THE RESERVATION AS A SCHOOL

The Anishinaabe people know of a story about two ghosts, the *jeebiwaag*.[87] In the story, an Anishinaabe *inini* (man) and his wife lived in a lodge far from other people. Each day, the *inini* left the lodge to hunt, while his wife remained home and handled duties around the lodge. Together, they made a comfortable home. The man's hunting provided the basic meat for sustenance, and the woman's (likely much greater) work provided a home. The man's hunting continued to be fruitful even as the snows of winter reached the lodge. But one day that winter, the Anishinaabe *kwe* (woman) noticed two pale figures sitting quietly, almost unnoticed in the darkest corner of the lodge. They looked emaciated, gaunt, like *jeebiwaag* (ghosts). The Anishinaabe *inini* arrived home with fresh meat, and the Anishinaabe *kwe* pointed out the two spooky figures sitting quietly in the corner. For they were spooky, very spooky. But the *jeebiwaag* did nothing, and so the Anishinaabe couple cooked a meal made from the fresh meat harvested that day, all the while watching the two pale figures in the corner to see what would happen. As the meat cooked, and the fat began to bubble and fizzle, the two *jeebiwaag* jumped out suddenly from the corner, tearing meat from the spit. They ate greedily, noisily, and ate all the best, fattiest parts of the meat. After the *jeebiwaag* had their fill, they retreated to the corner again, saying nothing. The Anishinaabe couple watched the *jeebiwaag* eat and then return to their corner, shocked and a little bit terrified. But they were Anishinaabe people, and they had guests, so they satisfied themselves with what food was left. No one said anything that night. The couple cleaned their lodge, stored what little food remained, and settled down for the night. The *jeebiwaag* sat quietly and did nothing. No one slept that night.

In the morning, the Anishinaabe *inini* left for the day's work and hunt. He regretted leaving his wife with the *jeebiwaag*, who were still there, but the day was bitter cold and it was snowing. If he didn't hunt, there would be no meat for dinner that night. The *jeebiwaag* had cleaned them out. Again, despite the terrible weather, the *inini* enjoyed a successful hunt. Meanwhile, that whole day, the Anishinaabe *kwe* performed her work around the house, all the while being observed by the quiet and pale *jeebiwaag*, the whole time being polite and a little bit creeped out by her guests. Again, the *jeebiwaag* just sat there, doing nothing, making no noise. The *inini* returned with fresh meat. The family cooked the meat, and as it began to sizzle, the *jeebiwaag* rushed from their spot in the corner. They grabbed hot meat from the spit and ripped the sinew from the bone with their teeth, chewing as hungrily and greedily as the day before, again eating all of the best portions, leaving little for the Anishinaabe couple. As they had before, the couple ate what was left, cleaned up, and went to bed. No one said anything.

The process repeated itself day after day for weeks on end as the harsh winter continued. Each day, the Anishinaabe *inini* left the lodge to harvest fresh meat and was amazingly successful, a miracle given the terrible winter. Each day, the Anishinaabe *kwe* performed her work at home, always under the watchful eyes of the *jeebiwaag*. They continued to sit in the corner, pale, gaunt, and completely silent, until the couple cooked their evening meal. Then, each night, the *jeebiwaag* tore the best meat from the spit and ate to excess. Each night, the Anishinaabe couple completed their evening routine and went to bed, two *jeebiwaag* living right there in the lodge with them.

Over time, the Anishinaabe *kwe* began to lose patience with this situation. It was one thing to host guests during the winter months, but these guests contributed nothing, and they took far more than they should have, every day. Day after day, as weeks passed, her irritation grew, until one evening, after the *jeebiwaag* had again consumed the best and fattiest portions of the meat, the Anishinaabe *kwe* lost her temper. She verbally lashed out at the *jeebiwaag*, demanding to know what they were doing there, day after day, eating all the best food, then sitting around all the rest of the time contributing nothing. The Anishinaabe *inini* apologized to the *jeebiwaag* profusely and tried to calm down his wife.

Finally, the *jeebiwaag* spoke. They explained they were in fact ghosts. They lived in the villages beyond the *jeebiziibi* (the river of death), and the Anishinaabe people there deeply resented the living. The dead Anishinaabeg believed the living Anishinaabeg were selfish and greedy and rude, unwilling to share their bounty with the dead. The two *jeebiwaag* chose to return to the world of the living to confirm the suspicions of the dead. They anticipated it would take three months to determine if the Anishinaabe people were living the right way. And the *jeebiwaag* were pleasantly surprised by the Anishinaabe couple. Instead of living selfish, mean lives, these living Anishinaabe were selfless and giving, they worked hard, and they treated visitors with respect. The *jeebiwaag* then apologized to the Anishinaabe *kwe* for their behavior, admitting that they were testing the Anishinaabe couple, and that they had taken the test too far. They said they had learned all they needed to learn in just six weeks, not the three months they were allotted, and decided to depart. The living Anishinaabe people had passed the test of the *jeebiwaag*.

I like to think this is a story about Mino-Bimaadiziwin, about living the right way. One lives the right way by treating others with respect and humility, for example – two of the Seven Grandmother (or Grandfather) teachings. I grew up in a home where guests were the priority. As soon as one enters an Anishinaabe home as a guest, they can expect to be offered a drink and a meal, even when there is little or nothing to be had. The Anishinaabe couple were fortunate in their lives, always having food and shelter, even in the dead of winter. They shared what they had with their guests, even these creepy *jeebiwaag*. They shared without really even understanding why. They lived in line with their teachings, and so they prospered.

Even the *jeebiwaag*, in their aggressive (and passive-aggressive) way, ultimately acknowledged those teachings. They had been mistaken about the living Anishinaabe people, growing envious and angry. During the time they called the test, they acted poorly, taking resources from their hosts without thanks, without making their own contributions, without living the right way. But in the end, they apologized. They admitted their error and demonstrated they hadn't forgotten their teachings. If anything, the dead Anishinaabeg were the ones who had forgotten the teachings. The *jeebiwaag* returned back to the lands beyond the river of death, back to their own world.

Indian people living with respect for their teachings are usually taught the right way to live and be by doing rather than by dictating in the abstract. Too often, non-Indians historically took that way of doing things as a sign of weakness, even of idiocy. During the middle part of the nineteenth century, as the federal–tribal relationship settled into a reservation system, the federal government began to assert control over how Indian people would live. As Indian people began to adapt to the new reservation style of living, no easy feat to be sure, non-Indians too often decided that these Indian adaptations were sure to fail. Non-Indians administering the reservation described the reservation as a school, a place where non-Indian people would teach Indian people how to live civilized lives. Indian people living, or attempting to live, on the reservation with an eye toward harvesting only natural resources needed for immediate needs and with an eye toward sustainability faced the dictates of non-Indians instructing them differently.

Reservation agents and superintendents began to dominate Indian lives, often in absurd ways. For example, without congressional authorization or even funding (at first), reservation officials established Indian courts, Indian police, and law and order codes.[88] This was during the era in which the United States, when it dealt with Indians and tribes at all, treated Indians as children, as wards of the federal government, which was the guardian. Under a guardianship, the guardian has enormous power over the ward. A parent is a guardian, a child is a ward. The whole idea behind guardianship law is that the ward is not legally competent. The ward cannot make legally binding decisions on their own, and it is the guardian's job to make those decisions for them. These are often financial decisions, but also decisions about every aspect of life, potentially. When Homer Simpson tells his kids he owns them like chattel property, he's not far off.

American Indian affairs from the founding to the early decades of the twentieth century constitute the guardianship period in the federal–tribal relationship. In the 1880s – possibly the worst decade for Indian people – the United States delved deeply into the contours of this guardianship. Keep in mind, federal *guardianship* over Indian people has little or no legal basis. Yes, there are more than four hundred Indian treaties, and in these treaties Indians and tribes agreed to come under the "protection" of the United States, not unlike how the Vatican is under the protection of Italy (by virtue of its location in Rome), Switzerland (through the Swiss Guard), and NATO, for that matter (again, by virtue of its location in western Europe). No one in their right mind would agree that Switzerland has authority to instruct the pope on how to do pope things. But that duty of protection the United States undertook justified, at least from the federal government's perspective, a guardianship style of Indian country governance. Instead of ensuring that Indian people and their tribes remained protected, the federal government just took over tribal government, tribal assets, and Indian lives.

What this meant at places like the Umatilla Indian reservation in northeastern Oregon was that the Office of Indian Affairs of the Department of the Interior created a weirdly diabolical scheme to control Indians. The Department of the Interior had crafted a generic reservation law and order code not unlike any municipal ordinance governing a small town. But like any municipal ordinance, the generic reservation law-and-order code was spiked with non-Indian morality and values. The Umatilla reservation Indians likely had never formally regulated social activities like marriage in a written code (and certainly not in English). Nor had Indians typically criminalized American social no-no's such as adultery. Nor had they criminalized their own religious practices. The federal government's law and order codes usually did all of these things, in addition to formally codifying a set of criminal prohibitions, another non-Indian introduction to Indian lives.

The Umatilla tribal nation is a confederacy of sorts, a federally created combination of three tribal groups, the Umatilla, Cayuse, and Walla Walla people, who all signed a treaty with the United States in 1855.[89] At the Umatilla Indian Reservation in the 1870s, the local Indian agent created a Court of Indian Offenses, which was the term at the time for tribal courts used all around the country. The Indian agent typically would staff the tribal court with Indian people as judges, police, and jailers. So at Umatilla, there was the court, the judge, a police officer who also served as a prosecutor, and a jail. All of these formal institutions were new to the reservation, as was the law and order code the Indian agent required the Court of Indian Offenses to enforce.

The federally imposed regime at Umatilla, like pretty much all other reservations on which this was dumped, was a poor fit, to say the least. The modern tribal government's website (in 2018) describes the traditional leadership structure as reliant on elders, appointed headmen who demonstrated special leadership skills at an early age:

> Individual abilities were recognized by elders at an early age. Headmen and chiefs were selected based upon their experience, abilities and skills. Elders were respected and often leaders had council with elders. Individuals were recognized for their spiritual strength, medicinal abilities, warrior qualities, recognized for their hunting and tracking abilities, fishing skills, art, weaving, education, discipline, healing, cooking or other skills. Labor and skills were divided as many survival skills were necessary.

A council of elders and appointed leaders would meet to make important decisions and to resolve disputes based on a consensus model:

> Conflicts and issues were resolved by council of elders and leaders. Leaders were decisive when they believed that their followers had arrived at a consensus. If there was no consensus, powerful orations between the headmen and chiefs might soon swing the people on issues or problems of the day.

> If an individual disagreed with the decisions of the band, he did not, nor was he forced to comply with the decision. Overall decisions of the Tribe were arrived at by

consensus of the people. Planning and preparations were conducted in ways to prepare for future generations.

In some ways, important ways, these statements from the tribe's website are vague generalities, platitudes. But they are clear enough to show that the Umatilla tribes did not govern with a ruthless top-down structure, unlike the governmental monopoly on violence Americans grow up learning to expect and too often fail to critique or question unless that system comes crashing down on their own heads. The way the modern Umatilla tribal government describes its historical and traditional government structure is pretty much how Anishinaabe Indian tribes would describe their own historical and traditional government structure.

The court in *United States v. Clapox*,[90] an 1888 decision from the federal district court in Oregon, perfectly described the way the Umatilla Court of Indian Offenses operated inside the reservation and the way the federal government's awesome law enforcement powers interacted. The federal judge in that case, Matthew Deady, a pioneer who literally walked the Oregon Trail as a young man in the late 1840s, also took the time in his opinion to editorialize about the purpose of Indian reservations, the contours of federal Indian policy, and his views on the inherent shortcomings of Indian people, all of it classic Indian-hating.

The *Clapox* case began when an Umatilla reservation resident named Minnie was arrested for "cohabiting" with an Indian man who was not her husband. Let that sink in, twenty-first century readers. America used to toss adulterers in jail. And late-nineteenth Americans in power, almost exclusively white men, focused on cultural, religious, and ethnic minorities. Federal officials charged with administering Indian affairs at that time obsessed over informal marriages and divorces by Indian people. If an Indian person cohabitated with another Indian person, then left that person for another without formal notification to anyone, let alone some Indian agent, that Indian agent might write a report about that Indian person, alleging polygamy or adultery. A key part of the American civilization project at that time, and throughout much of American history, was to control Indian family relations.[91] That was the core project of the law and order code and the Courts of Indian Offenses.

Judge Deady made that patently clear in his opinion. The federal government did not charge Clapox and his codefendants with adultery or polygamy. They didn't have to – Clapox and his conspirators were arrested trying to break Minnie out of a tribal jail, the crime of rescue, which is a federal crime – then and now. And we know Minnie was in that tribal jail for adultery. Deady began his opinion with a quotation from the federal law criminalizing breaking people out of jail but turned quickly to a detailed description of the Umatilla law and order code. Helpfully, Judge Deady described several of the offenses, none of which could be crimes under the current understanding of the US Constitution, but which were crimes the federal government wanted prosecuted in Indian country in the 1880s:

> Nos. 4, 5, 6, 7, and 8 of said rules prescribe the punishment for certain acts called therein "Indian offenses," such as the "sun," the "scalp," and the "war-dance," polygamy, "the usual practices of so-called medicine men," the destruction or theft of Indian property, and buying or selling Indian women for the purpose of cohabitation.[92]

In these words, Judge Deady described the religious activities in which Indian people throughout large portions of the West engaged: the sun dance, war dances, scalp dances, polygamy, prostitution, you name it. There's nothing in there, actually, about adultery, so apparently the Umatilla Court of Indian Offenses charged Minnie with polygamy or perhaps with "selling" herself for the "purposes of cohabitation." As I write this, federal prosecutions of people for religious activities are flatly unconstitutional under the Free Exercise Clause and illegal under the Religious Freedom Restoration Act.[93] Prostitution is illegal in almost all states, and while polygamy is also illegal, that practice is at least protected in some areas by lack of local prosecution (looking at you, rural Utah and Idaho).

But these crimes should not have detained Judge Deady, who was there to address the crime of jailbreak. He had to, though, because the defendant Clapox argued that the Court of Indian Offenses conviction was illegal in that no federal statute authorized the Indian agent to create the Court of Indian Offenses or promulgate the law and order codes. Moreover, Clapox argued, polygamy wasn't a crime at common law, and wasn't then (and isn't now) a federal crime at all. In other words, the legal predicate for Minnie's jailing was categorically invalid, meaning that Clapox and his associates were in the right in trying to break her out of jail.

Judge Deady knew all about bringing American law to the lawless West. He was a legislator in the Oregon Territory, and lead drafter of the Oregon Constitution, all by the 1850s. He later became a territorial judge and then, of course, a federal judge. He is credited with helping to codify Oregon's law. He knew all about American common law, and also criminal law. So he would have known that it was folly to criminalize sexual relations, not that the folly of doing so stops American legislatures, even today, from making the effort.

As a leader of the Oregon Territory, and then the state of Oregon, Judge Deady was familiar with the fact that there were Indian people in Oregon. Like a lot of pioneers, he probably came to this knowledge loaded with presuppositions about Indian people, namely that they weren't capable of managing their own affairs. An Indian agent assigned to Umatilla wrote that Judge Deady's impression of the Department of the Interior's administration of Indian trader regulations was "villainy made easy."[94] That, and Indian people were savages.

Judge Deady, in his *Clapox* opinion, explicitly and implicitly made five claims that detain me here. The first claim was that Indian people are savages. The second claim was that, as savages, Indian people cannot manage their own lives. The third claim was that the Umatilla reservation tribes consented to allow the federal government to manage the lives of Umatilla Indian people. The fourth claim was that the federal government's establishment of superintendency over the Umatilla reservation is in fulfillment of the obligation to manage the lives of Indian people. The fifth claim was that the federal government is authorized by the US Constitution and the Umatilla treaty to create the Court of Indian Offenses and its attendant offices and powers. It is plausible – even probable – that no more than two of these claims is correct, not just as a normative principle, but as a legal fact.

It is possible, arguable, that none of these claims is accurate. Let's take them in reverse order.

Federal Indian law supports the notion that the officials of the Department of the Interior were authorized by federal law to establish the Courts of Indian Offenses, but it's a close call. When the Office of Indian Affairs, the national office then and now (it's the Bureau of Indian Affairs now) charged with administering Indian affairs, first began to establish the Courts of Indian Offenses, no act of Congress or Indian treaty specifically authorized the creation of these courts. That's a big deal. Ask any conservative American if the federal government can take action outside of the express words of the Constitution and you are likely going to hear a resounding "No!" They're probably thinking of laws like the Affordable Care Act or the power of the president to set aside federal public lands as national parks. They're probably not thinking about Indian affairs, but hardcore conservative jurists like Clarence Thomas are doing that thinking for them, and Justice Thomas sees almost no power in the federal constitution for Congress or the president to do much of anything in Indian affairs. The same was largely true back in the 1880s, that if the federal government took an action it could not trace to the Constitution directly, the US Supreme Court would strike down the law.

The exception, such as it is, both then and now for the Supreme Court is Indian law and policy. In an 1886 case quoted extensively by Judge Deady, *United States v. Kagama*,[95] a case involving members of the Yurok Tribe near the Hoopa Valley Indian Reservation in far northern California, the Supreme Court was ready to strike down the federal statute called the Major Crimes Act extending criminal jurisdiction to Indian country[96] because it couldn't find words in the Constitution that authorized Congress to pass criminal laws in Indian country. The federal government argued that the Commerce Clause authorized Congress to regulate all commerce, which includes any form of intercourse with any kind of commercial nexus, including criminal activity. In fact, in 1790, one of Congress' first acts in Indian affairs, was to enact a criminal law or two governing Indian country.[97] So, if the First Congress presumed it had the power to regulate Indian country crime under the Commerce Clause, the government argued ninety-five years later, then it must possess that power. The *Kagama*

Court, reading the Constitution with blinders on, disagreed. But it upheld the law anyway because it concluded that Indians were so weak and dependent that if the United States didn't assert itself as guardian, all the Indians would die off from murder, starvation, disease, and whatever else would kill the most pathetic and most incompetent people in America. Yes, that was our Supreme Court in 1886 – quoting Judge Deady quoting the *Kagama* Court: "These Indian tribes are the wards of the nation; they are communities dependent on the United States; dependent largely for their daily food; dependent for their political rights. They owe no allegiance to the states, and receive from them no protection."[98] That was the sanitized version. A few paragraphs earlier, the *Kagama* Court said exactly the same thing but with much more detail about the threats faced by Indian people and how weak and sorry they were back then:

> These Indian tribes are the wards of the nation. They are communities dependent on the United States, – dependent largely for their daily food; dependent for their political rights. They owe no allegiance to the states, and receive from them no protection. Because of the local ill feeling, the people of the states where they are found are often their deadliest enemies. From their very weakness and helplessness, so largely due to the course of dealing of the federal government with them, and the treaties in which it has been promised, there arises the duty of protection, and with it the power.[99]

The *Kagama* Court's views on Indian people suffered from the same empirical softness as Judge Deady's similar statements about the Umatilla Reservation residents. The people within and around the Hoopa Reservation, including the Hupa, Yurok, Klamath, Karuk, Tolowa, and other Indian tribes, were about as strong and self-reliant as any people in the world, having survived the massacres by whites during the California Gold Rush period; federal military control and abuses on the Hoopa reservation; slavery, which was endemic in California for decades before and after the Thirteenth Amendment;[100] and the fact that the US Senate never ratified eighteen Indian treaties negotiated with California tribes (and then never told them the treaties weren't ratified).[101] That's far from weak and dependent. This weakness and dependency language was about the source of federal power more than it was about actual Indian people. In a truly twisted way, the federal government in *Kagama* had manufactured an empirically weak justification for the exercise of federal power in Indian country, and the Supreme Court, not really knowing any better (or caring), took the government's word for it, accepted it by adopting an empirically incorrect justification as constitutional fact.

That made Judge Deady's job a lot easier a few years later when Umatilla Indians from Oregon complained the government didn't have the power to criminally prosecute reservation Indians for things like adultery. The US Supreme Court, no less, had, as a matter of law, classified Indian people as incompetents requiring the protection of a guardian, which had to be the United States because states and their citizens couldn't be trusted to do it. If Congress could enact the Major Crimes Act, Judge Deady concluded, then the Office of Indian Affairs could establish law and order codes and create Courts of Indian Offenses to enforce the codes.

Judge Deady did look around for another source of authority, to his credit. He settled on the Umatilla treaty, the Treaty of Walla Walla, as a possible source of federal authority to create the Court of Indian Offenses. That treaty includes fairly unusual language in the world of Indian treaties: the tribes agreed to "submit to and observe all laws, rules, and regulations which may be prescribed by the United States for the government of said Indians."[102] Judge Deady asserted the treaty "obviously" authorized the federal action, sliding over the problem that Congress had not enacted a law authorizing the Courts of Indian Offenses, which of course was the source of the legal controversy. *Obviously*, any legal writing instructor will tell you, is an intensifier, an indication to a reader like me that the writer is papering over a weak point in the argument, ironically by highlighting that point. Yes, the Department of the Interior promulgated the law and order code as a regulation, but as any conservative legal commentator would observe, federal agencies cannot establish valid regulations without express authorization from Congress. Unhappily for Indian people chafing under the law and order codes and the Court of Indian Offenses, Congress did sort of ratify the codes and courts by appropriating funds to manage the courts going forward, starting later in 1888, after the *Clapox* situation arose. In sum, yes, federal law likely did authorize creation of the law and order codes and the Courts of Indian Offenses, under a broad reading of congressional and executive branch powers in Indian affairs. But under a more conservative interpretation of federal powers, maybe not so much.

Judge Deady's fourth claim in the *Clapox* opinion was that the enforcement of the law and order codes by the Court of Indian Offenses was doing the work of civilizing Umatilla Indians. Clapox and associates argued that the Court of Indian Offenses, under the thumb of the Indian agent, had the power to hold Indians indefinitely without basic due process, complaining

> that no written warrants are issued by said court, and no written record is kept of its findings or judgments; that under the rules establishing said court and police, and the direction of said agent, the officers of said police force had then and there the authority to arrest any Indian whom they might have cause to believe had "committed a crime or an Indian offense" on said reservation, and commit him to jail for examination or trial before said court.[104]

No warrants. No written records. The written rules – that is, the law and order code – allowed the court to detain an Indian indefinitely before trial. All of this under the eye of the Indian agent, who forced the court, the Indian police (who was also the prosecutor), and the law and order code on the people of the Umatilla Reservation. Clapox was arguing that this is no way served justice on the reservation, or anywhere.

No matter to Judge Deady. He wrote that this regime was part of a broad plan, part and parcel of guardianship, to teach Indians how to govern:

These "courts of Indian offenses" are not the constitutional courts provided for in section 1, art. 3, Const., which congress only has the power to "ordain and establish," but mere educational and disciplinary instrumentalities, by which the government of the United States is endeavoring to improve and elevate the condition of these dependent tribes to whom it sustains the relation of guardian.[105]

These Courts of Indian Offenses, Deady wrote, were certainly not adult courts like Article III courts (federal courts, that is), so quit your worrying. They were like playground courts, teaching Indians right from wrong and the contours of justice. Except, of course, these courts were cloaked in federal power, and therefore possessed the power to jail people. And to rescue someone from that jail was a federal crime.

Deady confirmed the classic, Indian-hating view of guardianship of Indians in the next sentence, where he stated that the entire reservation is a playpen in which Indian children could learn how to manage their own lives under the watchful eye of the federal guardian: "In fact, the reservation itself is in the nature of a school, and the Indians are gathered there, under the charge of an agent, for the purpose of acquiring the habits, ideas, and aspirations which distinguish the civilized from the uncivilized man."[106] What a school! Jail time without written charge. Indefinite detention without trial. Laws written by foreigners, imposing foreign values. Seems like hell, not unlike the boarding schools for Indian children the same foreigners forced upon Indian country.[107] Deady waved it away, suggesting that since the Indians were just beginning their march toward civilization, horrendous human rights violations were mere steps on the learning curve: "From this Indian court and police, in this, their first effort in the administration of justice, written process and proceedings could not have been expected."[108]

And what about those values, those "habits, ideas, and aspirations"? Judge Deady turned clever, labeling "plural marriages . . . peculiar to the Indian in his savage state."[109] Deady was sloppy here, because adultery and polygamy aren't really the same thing – in fact categorically not the same thing. Still, it was reasonable, in Deady's view, for the federal government to criminalize adultery in Indian country in order to stamp out the uncivilized practice. And Indians who violate federally imposed moral obligations are guilty of a federal crime.

Adultery is the underlying charge, remember, and that wasn't really a crime even in late-nineteenth-century America, and it definitely wasn't a federal crime. It was a crime in England, where they had ecclesiastical courts, or church courts, because they didn't have the separation of church and state as in the United States. Deady sloughed that off, saying some American states and localities did criminalize adultery, and the federal government was just acting as a state or locality would, but in Indian country. Deady was sloppy here, too. Adultery was the child's crime. Rescue was the adult's crime. What the hell is the federal government doing?

In the end, Judge Deady impliedly acknowledged the low comedy of it all. He concluded his opinion by invoking the satire of the seventeenth-century magistrate of New Amsterdam, Wouter Van Twiller, made famous by Washington Irving:

> The old Knickerbocker, Wouter van Twiller, when exercising the office of magistrate, paid no heed to parchment, but delivered to the constable, as the symbol of his authority, his well-known jack-knife and tobacco box, armed with which the Dogberry of New Amsterdam might safely "comprehend all vagrom men."[110]

Magistrate Van Twiller, in Irving's telling, was so fat and lazy he would listen to a constable's statement about probable cause while munching his breakfast. Instead of issuing a written summons and a warrant, Van Twiller was known to hand over his jackknife and tobacco box to the constable, which was apparently sufficient to compel the appearance of the subject before the magistrate. What a joke, along the lines of saying that if warrantless arrests and the lack of a written record were good enough for the people of New Amsterdam, they were good enough for Indians. Funny, surely, to Judge Deady. Not so much to the people of Umatilla.

The federal government's guardianship of Indian people was a strange matter, leading to strange decisions. The *Clapox* debacle might be among the strangest. And most heartbreaking. As an outsider to Umatilla Indian people, I don't know much about the tragedy of Minnie, but something tells me it deserves a better telling than Judge Deady's open mockery. The ironic thing is that the Umatilla Indian Tribe was among the first three tribes to implement the tribal jurisdiction provisions under the 2013 Violence Against Women Reauthorization Act that allowed Indian tribes to prosecute non-Indians for dating and domestic violence.[111] In order to assert this power, the Umatilla tribal government has to guarantee a higher overall standard of criminal procedure rights to the non-Indian defendants than they would receive in state and federal courts. In some respects, perhaps, the legacy of the federal government's ridiculous guardianship is that the Umatilla government, which is a government of the Umatilla people, gave teeth to their respect for individual rights.

Indian tribes and Indian people are doing the right things for the right reasons, or at least trying to. What is happening in Indian country could be a function of higher values. Judge Deady seemed to be writing from the perspective of the beneficiary of a quasi-feudal system, where elites ruled without compassion or wisdom and without ever having to face an accounting from normal people.

I keep returning to the Anishinaabe story of the two *jeebi* who tested the Anishinaabe family. The *jeebiwaag* imposed the test in a sort of bad faith and behaved horribly. Through all of this, however, the Anishinaabe couple kept living their lives in accordance with their values, in Mino-Bimaadiziwin. They showed humility, generosity, and patience. And in the end it was the *jeebiwaag* who learned the biggest lesson and showed actual remorse.

I don't know about Minnie, or her lover, or Clapox, and whether Clapox was Minnie's lover, but I know a little bit how the federal government – and Judge Deady – tested them. The government came to this test in bad faith, and Judge Deady made sure the government wouldn't have to learn anything. But I imagine the Umatilla people learned a great deal, internalized right and wrong, civilized from uncivilized, and found that their guardian was the uncivilized one.

7

BABY STEALING (ANCIENT)

The Anishinaabe people know stories about young people who mysteriously fall sick and walk on into the world of the dead – but they are not dead.[112] In one story told by the people of Waganakising (the traditional name for an important village affiliated with the Little Traverse Bay Bands of Odawa Indians), a young Anishinaabe *inini* (man) named Betosegay (usually now Americanized into the name Petoskey), who was betrothed to a young Anishinaabe *kwe* (woman) named Wenona, fell ill and collapsed. He was the strongest of the young men of Waganakising, with the finest hunting and sporting skills.

Wenona, along with Betosegay's mother, Nokoqua, watched over him, but he did not emerge from his coma. Then, suddenly, Betosegay rose from his bed, shrieked a piercing scream, and walked out the door of the lodge. Wenona and Nokoqua jumped up and followed him out the door, calling his name, but he would not respond. They followed him, but he kept walking quickly away from the lodge, heading west. No matter how much they ran, they could not keep up with him. They kept calling and calling, but Betosegay kept moving away from them supernaturally fast, seeming to hover above the trail into the woods. Eventually, Wenona, tired and despairing, stopped her chase, but Nokoqua continued. Exhausted and spent, she lost sight of her son in the night. But she continued onward anyway.

Nokoqua knew her Anishinaabe teachings and realized she was heading west on the *jeebikana* (ghost road), toward the world of the dead Anishinaabe. But she would not stop. She believed it was not time for her Betosegay to walk on to the next world, and she would continue onward, no matter how hopeless matters seemed, to bring him back. She walked through the dark woods, barely able to see the trail. She walked and walked until she began to hear a rushing sound. The sound grew louder and louder as she approached. She realized this sound was the *jeebiziibi* (the river of death). As she approached the river, she saw a massive dead tree splayed out over the water, ostensibly the bridge over the river of the dead. The tree was very old and rotted, and the footing looked treacherous. Then she saw the river itself, which gave off a thunderous sound. The water rushed powerfully down a steep gorge, and the river twisted viciously through the forest, like a snake. She could see that to fall in this river would mean being lost forever.

A little ways up the river, Nokoqua saw a small lodge. She approached and knocked on the door. A Mishomis (grandfather) opened the doorway and started when he saw Nokoqua. "*Aaniin*, sister," Mishomis said in greeting. Nokoqua asked the Mishomis for help, but he shook his head.

"You don't belong here."

"My son, Betosegay, came through here. I want to find him and bring him home."

The elder Anishinaabe *inini* (man) nodded. "I saw him. He walked right past me." The Mishomis explained that it was his job to warn the newly deceased Anishinaabe people, some of whom didn't realize they were dead, about the river of death and the passage over the bridge. Apparently Betosegay was still alive, but he walked so quickly that Mishomis couldn't stop him and send him back. He agreed to help Nokoqua. But he warned her, the longer they stayed in the world of the dead, the more torment they would suffer. Their living minds were not prepared for death. The journey ahead would be extremely difficult.

The Mishomis told Nokoqua that she must not fall into the river of the dead. He pointed with his lips over to a sight that disturbed Nokoqua more than anything she had ever seen in the world of the living. There was a deceased Anishinaabe Benodjehn, a baby, still wrapped snuggly in a *tiginaagan* (cradleboard), struggling to cross the bridge over the river of death. The Benodjehn fell into the river. "They never make it," the Mishomis said sadly. "You see minnows in the rivers where you live? Those are the Anishinaabe Benodjehn who were lost in the river of the dead."

Nokoqua shuddered. But she was ever more determined to cross the river and save her own Benodjehn. She carefully maneuvered over the dangerous and rickety deadfall and reached the other side. The Mishomis waved at her and she moved on.

Nokoqua walked along the trail, the woods becoming deeper and darker. She walked for three days. Again she came to a clearing, a village, with many, many lodges set close to each other at the far end of the clearing. It was finally morning. There were songbirds out. The air smelled fresh and clean. One lodge, close to where Nokoqua emerged from the forest, was set apart. A Nokomis (grandmother) emerged from the lodge, smiling broadly at first. But then her smile fell as she realized Nokoqua was not dead. "You shouldn't be here," the Nokomis said.

"I've come to retrieve my son," Nokoqua said. "His name is Betosegay, and he is not dead, either."

The Nokomis nodded. "I have seen him. He passed by here yesterday. He is here somewhere in the village. And he is in great pain."

Nokoqua was both relieved and horrified. "Can you help me?"

The Nokomis said she would try. "We must be quick. After the fourth day, your son will not be allowed to leave."

They waited, and after a time several Anishinaabe people walked out from the forest on the other side of the village. They were laughing and talking. Many of them had horrid injuries, missing limbs, smallpox scars, or other disfigurements. Others looked emaciated and ill. Still others looked exactly like an Anishinaabe person would look in life. But no matter what their physical body looked like, they were talking and singing as they entered the village clearing. Some of them began setting up a drum and began to sing. Others began to dance. The scene was beautiful. The dead Anishinaabeg were at peace.

Except for one. Betosegay came in with the dead Anishinaabe. But he was holding his head in his hands and moaning horribly. Nokoqua gasped. Betosegay truly was suffering. She rushed to him and tried to grab his hand, to hug him, but he acted like she wasn't even there.

Then Nokomis walked over. She reached for Betosegay's hand and brought it over to Nokoqua's hand. She joined them. Only then did Betosegay come out of his trance, his pain.

"Niimaamaa?" Betosegay said as he recognized his mother. They embraced for a time.

"You must go now," the Nokomis said sternly. "Before it is dark."

The shadows were lengthening across the clearing. Nokoqua and Betosegay walked east through the forest. They seemed to be traveling much more quickly, Nokoqua thought. Before long, they reached the river of death. The Mishomis on the other side waved urgently to them.

"Hurry," he called, "before the sun sets."

Nokoqua and her son crossed the bridge over the river of the dead. They thanked the old Mishomis and hurried home. The forest became darker and darker, but they traveled on. Eventually, they reached the end of the forest and saw their village. It was morning.

The worst horror human beings face is the possible loss of a child. Indian people are no different. But the number of lost children Indian people have suffered is incredible, virtually impossible to comprehend. In Michigan, Anishinaabe families have lost far too many children in every generation going back centuries – literally centuries. Almost all of these losses are attributable to European and American Indian-hating disguised as sympathetic pleas for reform.

Many American statements of Indian-hating in the nineteenth century were offered in this way. This variety of Indian-hating came as words in support of trying to save Indian people from themselves. Consider *A Plea for the Papoose*, General Thomas Jefferson Morgan's address to an Albany, New York, audience in 1892 while he was commissioner of Indian Affairs.[113] Morgan began by entreating his audience to consider that Indian babies were just like Christian babies (mostly): "Indian nature is human nature bound in red."[114] Still, Morgan, the sympathetic-to-Indians reformer, betrayed shocking racism: "Undoubtedly there is much in heredity[,] much in the race differences between the Mongolian and the Caucasian, and between these and the African and the Indian."[115] Morgan, speaking from the point of view of the unspeaking "papoose," advocated for equal educational opportunities. If education failed Indian people, Morgan's "papoose" conceded, "we accept whatever position of inferiority may be forced upon us by any lack inherent in our natures."[116]

Morgan's final line of attack was to invoke for his American audience the threat uneducated, uncivilized, un-Christian Indians would pose to America. General Morgan seemingly invoked his national security expertise by pointing out that attempting to educate Indians was good for "their white neighbors as well."[117] Uneducated Indians, for Morgan, were a "menace":

> To leave these thousands of children to grow up in ignorance, superstition, barbarism, and even savagery, is to maintain a perpetual menace to our western civilization and to fasten upon the rapidly developing States of the West, an incubus that will hinder their progress, arrest their growth, threaten their peace, and be continually, as long as it remains, a source of unrest and of perplexity.[118]

Indian-hating like this is advocacy for social change in order to deal with an inherent liability, the mere existence of Indian children, to future American generations. In the latter half of the nineteenth century and well into the twentieth, the federal government forced Indian children into military-style boot-camp industrial schools or Christian missionary boarding schools. Americans used physical abuse, isolation from family, ideological and religious indoctrination, poor housing and health care, and too many other manners of uncivilized education to destroy Indian culture and languages. It was horrifically efficient. Just as Morgan wanted, Indian children lost much of what made them Indian, which for Morgan was by definition a "menace" to America.

American policy makers like Morgan considered Indian children to be a liability. They were a threat, an untenable cost center for western states at a time when America's westward expansion dominated the country's culture and politics.

The Anishinaabe stories about the *jeebiziibi* are instructive. Indian people can get lost, can be taken across the river of the dead, but they are not dead. Taking those Indian children away from their mothers and fathers, their grandparents, their cousins and aunties and uncles, their friends and their language, their culture – that would be like death. Americans took Indian children to boarding schools to kill the Indian parts of them, but they just threw Indian children into the river, a river from which there was no escape, from which those Indian Benodjehn would lose everything that made them Indian, that made them human. I think of the Anishinaabe teaching on the minnows when I think of the ancestors taken by the Americans.

Luckily, Indian people never gave up. Like Nokoqua, they continued to walk down the path, even if it was a path of death, always trying to bring back their loved ones, their children.

When I go to Indian law conferences, or stare out at my Indian law classes, I think about those minnows we lost. I think about the work we are doing to stop the bleeding of our future generations. I hope we are making those ancestors that walked the path of death proud.

PART 2
MODERN INDIAN-HATING

THEORIES ON SUPERSESSION AND ANTI-SUPERSESSION

Minnesota Ojibwe people love to tell the story of why there are still pine forests in their homelands in Anishinaabewaki (the world of the Anishinaabe).[119] The American hero Paul Bunyan logged off all the old-growth timber in Michigan and Wisconsin. He stole the livelihoods of thousands of Anishinaabe people who depended on their woodlands for sustenance and trade. The Minnesota Anishinaabe heard Paul Bunyan crashing through, looking for white pine near Cass Lake. They passed on a signal to the *binewaag* (partridges), who passed on a signal to the *maanwaag* (loons), who passed on a signal to the hoofed creatures, the *makwaag* (bears), and the wildcats. All the animals signaled with their sounds, and Nanaboozhoo, the Anishinaabe hero and trickster, heard them and came quickly. He confronted Paul Bunyan just as the lumberjack had begun to cut down white pine forests. Nanaboozhoo told Paul Bunyan that the Anishinaabeg depended on the forests to live, but Paul Bunyan would not stop. For three days, they fought and argued. Finally, Nanaboozhoo reached down and pulled an *ogaa* (walleye) from a lake, and walloped Paul Bunyan in the face, knocking him out. Nanaboozhoo then shaved Paul Bunyan's whiskers and made a hat out of them. That's why there are still pine forests in parts of Minnesota Anishinaabewaki.

Indian peoples' dependence on their homelands cannot be underestimated. The vast forests that Europeans and Americans chopped down were the homes and livelihoods of hundreds of Indian cultures and communities. Indian people would have done anything then to stop that deforestation, just as they often now take action to stop more depredations upon their homelands.

That Indian people depended on the resources available to them in their homelands, and actually did what they could to make those resources sustainable, is too often antithetical to the American view that resources are to be exploited until exhausted. Indian advocacy in this area of thought sadly became a source of much Indian-hating.

In 1970, Martin Cruz Smith, long before he became the famous author of the Arkady Renko detective novels, published *The Indians Won*. The premise of the novel is an alternative history fantasy in which the Indians won, unifying effectively in the nineteenth century and stopping the Americans cold in their westward expansion. Much of the Great Plains and the Rocky Mountains is Indian Territory, completely closed off to Americans. The story takes place in the modern era where the Indian nation acquires a nuclear weapon and becomes a geopolitical player. It's not a story of Indian-hating, although it has a fair bit of squirm-inducing mischaracterizations of Indian people. Martin Cruz Smith probably was no Indian-hater, but he wrote about a bountiful source of Indian-hating: the restoration of lands taken by Americans back to Indian people.

The fantasy – and it is a fantasy – of Indian tribes retaking back the whole of America, or much larger areas than they currently possess, is an old one. It is an idea that terrifies many non-Indians. The leaders of the Ghost Dance religion adopted by many Indian people in the late nineteenth century promised that supernatural forces would wipe out the Americans and bring back those lost to war, starvation, and disease. The idea contained in the Ghost Dance religion was so threatening to Americans that it was perhaps one of the instigators of the Wounded Knee massacre perpetrated by the Seventh Cavalry.

In 2007, some Indian people declared the independence of a Republic of Lakotah. The leaders of the Republic of Lakotah purported to formally withdraw from the 1851 and 1868 treaties between the United States and several Indian tribes.[120] That withdrawal would restore the independent national status of the Republic of Lakotah. The republic announced the restoration of the pretreaty borders, ostensibly reverting about half of five states – Montana, Wyoming, Nebraska, and the Dakotas – back to aboriginal (or pretreaty cession) land status.

There is good cause for Indian nations to assert treaty rights and to reassess the foundational facts underlying their treaties. The United States agreed to take Indian nations and Indian people under its protection in those treaties, and history shows the federal government failed miserably in its obligations. But there is good cause not to take seriously the Republic of Lakotah, not the least of which is that there are federally recognized Indian nations that are the actual parties to the 1851 and 1868 treaties. Those Indian nations are not withdrawing from the treaties. There are also hundreds of thousands of non-Indian people living within the territorial borders claimed by the Republic of Lakotah. In short, Indian and non-Indian people have justifiable reasons not to recognize it. Still, the Republic of Lakotah serves an important role in publicizing the status of Indian nations within the United States and forces Americans to acknowledge the continuing advocacy of Indian people in preserving their rights.

Modern Indian nations are resilient entities that are carving out a place within the American federalist system of government. They govern in light of their cultures and traditions. And they take seriously their obligations under the treaties and the trust relationship with the United States. For example, the Waganakising Odawa, the Little Traverse Bay Bands of Odawa Indians, adopted a tribal constitution that announces its commitment to its language, its culture, and the trust relationship:

> IN THE WAYS OF OUR ANCESTORS, to perpetuate our way of life for future generations, we the Little Traverse Bay Bands of Odawa Indians, called in our own language the WAGANAKISING ODAWAK, a sovereign, self-governing people who follow the Anishinaabe Traditions, Heritage, and Cultural Values, set forth within this Constitution the foundation of our governance. This Constitution is solemnly pledged to respect the individuality of all our members and their spiritual beliefs and

practices, while recognizing the importance of preserving a strong, unified Tribal identity in accordance with our Anishinaabe Heritage. We will work together in a constructive, cooperative spirit to preserve and protect our lands, resources and Treaty Rights, and the right to an education and a decent standard of living for all our people. In keeping faith with our Ancestors, we shall preserve our Heritage while adapting to the present world around us.

We have created this document as an act of inherent self-governance pursuant to the government-to-government relationship.[121]

The Waganakising Odawa statement of governance principles is an articulation of how modern American Indian nations strive to govern. This is not a statement of empire, or domination, or violence, or even a critique or attack on the United States for its historical treatment of the Odawa people. It is in this way a much different statement than, say, the Declaration of Independence, or the announcement of the establishment of the Republic of Lakotah. However, contemporary Western philosophy too often does not notice this nuance. The fantasy of total American Indian resurgence continues to dominate this area of thought.

One of the fundamental tenets of Indian-hating is opposition to the restoration of historical tribal property rights and governance. Possibly the most esoteric and theoretical argument against restoration of lands and financial reparations is antisupersession, the claim that to replace the current status of property ownership and governance with Indian or tribal ownership and governance on the basis of correcting historic justice is unjust.

Jeremy Waldron is a world-renowned legal and political philosopher, generally espousing liberal progressive ideas, who has argued for decades that the illegitimate taking of property and sovereignty from Indigenous peoples a century or more ago does not justify the restoration of the property and sovereignty to Indigenous peoples now. Waldron's argument is laid out in his 1992 essay, "Superseding Historic Injustice,"[122] published in the year in which most Westerners celebrated the five-hundred-year anniversary of the arrival of Christopher Columbus to the Americas. Waldon's argument is a narrow one, even a simple one, but it is intended to cut the heart out of the arguments made by Indigenous peoples, including Indians in the United States, favoring the restoration of their property and sovereignty. It is insidious Indian-hating.

Waldron's theoretical claims favoring one form of supersession and opposing another form of supersession suggest a mighty struggle against internal contradiction, one that Waldron docs not acknowledge. Objective observers will be forced to conclude that Waldron's theory cannot possibly survive its own weight. Further, the entire narrow argument rests on a series of false premises, falsities that we will see often recur in other arguments against Indian people and Indian tribes. Finally, and perhaps most regretfully, the argument is so permeated with ethnocentric bias as to undermine whatever moral force it might have.

Simply put, *supersession* is fancy word for replacement. *Supersession*, as understood by commentators that use the term, was what happened when (in the United States at least) colonizers and conquerors arrived, took almost all property owned or controlled by Indians and Indian tribes, and destroyed their societies, including their ability to self-govern. Put like this, supersession seems almost comically oversimplified. In using these terms to describe the United States, supersession theorists must live with the assumption that the replacement of Indians by non-Indians is over and done with. However, the apocalypse that beset Indians beginning in 1492 in what is now the United States is ongoing and diabolically ever-changing and amorphous. It was true then and throughout American history, it is true now, and it will be for the foreseeable future. Oversimplification of this injustice and the proposed remedies allows the oversimplified to gloss over difficulties with the argument and, worse, allows commentators to caricature their opponents. Oversimplification dooms supersession theories.

Donning the protective cloak of oversimplification, Waldron opposes remedying historic supersession with another round of supersession. Recall that supersession as described by Waldron effectively means the well-nigh magical and instantaneous replacement of one system of property ownership and governance by one group of people by another. Presumably, the principles behind the arguments against supersession have practical meaning, because no one in their right mind could even contemplate how supersession would actually work in the real world. Perhaps the only real-world examples are recent instances involving the armed invasion of a small, weak country by a powerful country with a massive, efficient army – the United States' invasions of Afghanistan and Iraq, for example. And maybe that is what happened, sort of, in the early stages of World War II as well. And yet, as you will see below, supersession is not what happened in the context of American Indian nations.

Still, let's begin with the assumption that supersession is a useful way to describe Indian and non-Indian relations throughout American history. Let's assume that all Indigenous governance and property rights gave way completely to invading conquerors and colonists. Waldron's core claim is that the supersession of the ancient property and governance rights of Indian people and Indian tribes, while a terrible injustice, is not a sufficient reason to make supersession of the contemporaneous property and governance rights of non-Indians just. Another way of putting it (my way, not Waldron's) is that supersession can *never* be just because there will always be victims of supersession who are innocent and have expectations that their property and governance rights will not be changed in order to correct harms they themselves did not create. Supersession means the stripping of property rights of non-Indians and turning those property rights over to Indians. Supersession means the disestablishment of non-Indian governments and replacing those governments with tribal governments.

Waldron admits that there is a significant moral hazard here, that the perpetrators of supersession would have every incentive to take and hold property and governance long enough to artificially create legal rights. But his answer to that moral hazard is really quite inadequate. Waldron agrees that the passage of time alone is not sufficient to justify antisupersession but instead suggests that changes in circumstances are sufficient. Waldron relies on an allegory of watering holes in the savanna (more on this and other hypotheticals later) to argue in favor of the changed circumstances justification. In this hypothetical, there are numerous separate groups that each have adequate access to watering holes even if they exercise the power of exclusion to enforce exclusive access to their water. Waldron suggests that this is just. But the twist is the changed circumstance of an ecological disaster that dries out all but one watering hole. If the owner of that watering hole refuses to allow the others access to the watering hole, that is unjust according to Waldron and can be remedied by supersession to ensure all have access to the remaining watering hole.

Waldron's savanna hypothetical misses the mark. At the time of first contact, there were few enough Indian people (especially after the European diseases killed millions of Indians) and non-Indian people that there were enough resources for all. But as more and more non-Indians appeared, they pushed Indian people out of many of the best locations. The better savanna analogy would be that the number of watering holes stayed the same, but that one group began to grow exponentially and unjustly forced out the owners of all the other watering holes, taking control over all of them. Modern Indian people just want their watering hole back, not all watering holes. Waldron's changed circumstances could not have justified the improper acquisition by non-Indians of all the watering holes at the expense of the original owners, and he doesn't say it does. But the argument suggests that over time non-Indian ownership and reliance on the stolen watering holes somehow justifies denying the restoration of ownership to Indians. Indians are not asking for all of the watering holes in the savanna, just the watering holes stolen from them.

There is an even more pernicious and unspoken lesson in Waldron's savanna hypothetical. The original owners of the stolen watering holes presumably have the option to access the watering holes, but only by joining the group that stole their resources and agreeing to comply with the rules these thieves have set down. In short, the price for Indians to access the resources they once owned is their self-determination – their culture, their language, their loyalties. Waldron's solution to the moral hazard problem he identifies is genocidal. Join your oppressors. Or die.

In sum, Waldron's supersession and antisupersession theories suffer from the internal contradiction that supersession is both just and unjust. Waldron acknowledges that the supersession *of* Indian people is unjust, but also argues that supersession *by* Indians is unjust. To paraphrase Orwell, some supersessions are more equal than others.

The second major flaw in Waldon's argument involves the two critical and false factual premises, that American Indian people exercised no powers of self-determination and possessed no property during the periods of time between the dispossession of property and sovereignty and their modern-day claims to property and sovereignty. In the first critique of Waldron's supersession theory, I granted Waldron's supersession premise. Here, I argue supersession is a straw man that Waldron attempts, unsuccessfully, as the previous pages show, to destroy.

At times in Waldron's thinking on these questions, he focuses on the Maori people of what is now New Zealand. But the conclusions he makes are described broadly to apply to all Indigenous peoples. Supersession is a caricature of the reality of Indian people, the complexity of which undermines all the foundations of Waldron's argument.

First, Indians and Indian tribes throughout American history owned and controlled millions of acres of land within American boundaries. On hundreds of Indian reservations, large and small, Indian property rights remained. Waldron's theory presupposes that Indian people went from owning everything to owning nothing, and that supersession requires massive property transfers. While Indian nations are always hoping to expand their land bases, no one outside of the Republic of Lakotah entity advocates for the wholesale transfer of entire states or regions, untold millions of square miles of non-Indian land, to Indian nations.

In the United States, at least, there is a process by which Indian nations can acquire new reservation lands, usually called the fee to trust process.[123] In this process, Indian nations acquire land on the open market, clear title and buy title insurance, perform federal environmental reviews, and then hope the secretary of the Department of the Interior agrees to take the land into federal ownership in trust for the tribe. The process allows for stakeholders to comment on proposed fee to trust transfers, and even to sue the secretary for violations of federal law or when they disagree with the secretary's decision. As a practical matter, Indian nations effectively have to buy their reservations back at five to ten times the price paid for them, if they can somehow navigate this highly politicized process. This is hardly supersession.

Another fundamental problem for Waldron is what sovereignty means to American Indians. Waldron tries to avoid thorny questions about the legitimacy and scope of sovereignty but grants the argument that Indian tribes possessed sovereignty, whatever that means. It seems Waldron is not convinced that Indian tribes possessed sovereignty, which he defines as requiring a monopoly on violence, but he is willing to let that one go, arguing that predispossession tribal sovereignty doesn't hurt his argument.

But it does, and fatally. What sovereignty is to the modern-day state, and to the state that dispossessed Indians and tribes of property and sovereignty (largely the same entity with the same characteristics), is not necessarily what sovereignty is for Indian people. A monopoly on violence? For predispossession Indians? Hardly. Many, if not most, of hundreds or perhaps thousands of Indian tribes were not governed from the top down on a regime based on violence or the threat of violence (many were, perhaps it is true). They governed by what could loosely be described as consensus. Predispossession tribal sovereignty usually looked a lot different from parallel non-Indian, Western European sovereignty upon which it is implied that Waldron bases his judgments. Modern tribal sovereignty, such as that advocated by the Waganakising Odawa, continues that tradition.

Even granting that the leaders of Indian nations – or other advocates who some call sovereignty warriors – preach a robust, Western form of tribal sovereignty does not mean supersession on the level that would concern Waldron, if he would admit to being concerned. Unlike high-level federal and state elected officials and political appointees, tribal leaders are not beholden to powerful outside interests. Tribal leaders don't get elected because they had the backing of powerful oil and gas interests. They don't get elected because of powerful financial institutions on Wall Street or because of Russian or Chinese interference or support. They get elected by their relatives and neighbors. And while the occasional tribal leader might act in a self-interested manner, tribal leaders do not do so to reward political donors. Indian nations don't invade other countries or work to undermine the democratic processes of other governments. Waldron says he won't worry about what sovereignty means for purposes of supersession, and he need not worry at all. Tribal sovereignty is uniquely tribal, not the sovereignty asserted by Western nations. In short, the second major flaw of Waldron's supersession claims are that supersession itself, as Waldron characterizes it, is fiction.

The third major flaw in Waldron's conception is the ethnocentrism inextricably tied into his argument. It goes beyond the simple tie-goes-to-the-innocent-owner position Waldron takes in the savanna hypothetical. The savanna hypothetical itself is relentlessly racist, explicitly invoking the Anglo-American stereotyping of Indigenous people as animals, savages living in a state of nature, always on the brink of mindless violence. In another hypothetical, this time comparing Indigenous peoples to a childlike, ignorant figure, Waldron invokes his aunt's investment strategies, which might or might not be rational, to question whether Maori people would have held on to their lands or sold them off given the choice. Indigenous people are the irrational actors Waldron uses his irrational aunt to mock. In yet another hypothetical (one he acknowledges isn't very useful, but he still advances it), Waldron supposes that entire generations of non-Indians would have to be killed in order to make right what has happened to Indians. The long history of Americans and others espousing the threat of violence and torture from Indigenous people in order to justify the destruction of Indian communities shows Waldron's hypothetical to have a clear meaning, a dog whistle even, to his non-Indian audience.[124]

There are plenty of real-world hypotheticals involving actual Indigenous people Waldron could have used; for example, the Black Hills in present-day South Dakota. The Black Hills is claimed as the sacred homeland of numerous tribes. In 1980, the Supreme Court acknowledged that the United States illegally confiscated the Black Hills from those tribes.[125] Much of the Black Hills today is federal and state public lands in which private citizens have relatively little economic interest. Restoration of the Black Hills to the tribes would be a massive political issue, but that's all. It's a real-world question worthy of Waldron's attention. Instead, Waldron offers watering holes on a savanna, the investments of a silly relative, and intergenerational murder of non-Indians. An intelligent and honest hypothetical could have addressed the legal, political, and economic consequences of restoring the federal public lands in the Black Hills region to the 1851 and 1868 treaty signatories who signed in order to preserve their ownership of those lands.

Waldron either doesn't know enough about real-world matters or doesn't care. His audience is not Indian people. In Waldron's analysis, supersession is always imposed by non-Indians on passive Indians. He falls into the same trap too many commentators do when discussing Indian people and Indian nations by assuming Indians have no agency of their own. Indians and tribes are now struggling and have always struggled to save their lands and their governance powers. There are currently more than 570 federally recognized Indian tribes, each exercising governmental powers over Indian lands. Complete supersession of Indians by non-Indians was always a fiction. Indian agency complicates the overly simple Waldron theory, which apparently is intended to persuade non-Indians of the safety and even justice of their ethical position in relation to Indians by establishing the straw man of total supersession.

Complete supersession by Indians over non-Indians is also a fantasy. Indian nations don't claim it. Indian people, almost all of whom have relationships with non-Indians, don't want it. The Republic of Lakotah, which arguably does both, is engaged in a useful political exercise, but that's all.

Historical injustice imposes injury that Waldron apparently cannot observe and therefore does not credit. It is my sense that Western thinkers compartmentalize cause and effect in a way that the Anishinaabeg do not. Anishinaabe philosophy is rooted in the linkages between things, not the separation. In his philosophical opus, *The Metaphysics of Modern Existence*, Vine Deloria, Jr. argued that Western philosophy too often separates time and space. American law, building on this philosophy, rejects or severely restricts remedies for historical injustices because Western philosophy cannot readily conceive how the actions of the dead continue to control the destiny of the living.

American scholars and observers who reported old Anishinaabe Nanaboozhoo stories, for example Henry Schoolcraft, couldn't help but believe that their American culture was killing the culture that spawned Nanaboozhoo. Schoolcraft even made up a story about how an irrelevant Nanaboozhoo left the Anishinaabe as American culture approached.[127] Consider how Schoolcraft might have reacted to the story of Nanaboozhoo defeating Paul Bunyan and saving the Minnesota pine forests. Indian people aren't going away. Indian culture and worldviews aren't going away.

9

DOG WHISTLES

The worst of curses in the Anishinaabe communities where I grew up involved the bear walk.[128] As a child, I would see my elders cringe when someone mentioned bear walk. The bear walk came from hate and jealousy. Imagine a person wronged by another because of adultery or theft. Imagine a person envious of another who has more possessions or a stronger family. A person who became angry at another person could let that anger fester, let the anger grow inside them, tear them apart from the inside out. Anger and jealousy can lead to hate. Anishinaabe people believed such a person could gain supernatural powers, a curse on themselves and others. They could become a bear walk. If an Anishinaabe person saw a bird near a window, they knew not to let that bird in. If the bird got in the house, someone close to them would die. If an Anishinaabe person saw a bright ball of light in the woods at night, a bear walk was on the move. Someone was going to die that night.

Manidowaag, spirits, or *matchimanidowaag*, bad spirits or monsters, are strong indicators of the issues that troubled the Anishinaabe in the past. For Michigan Indians, the bear walk was the manifestation of personal, even petty, disputes that could tear apart a small, insular community. Many Anishinaabe stories, including the origin story of Anishinaabewaki (the world of the Anishinaabe), warn against revenge.[129] Bear walk is the physical manifestation of revenge, a pure form of hate and jealousy.

There are more than 570 federally recognized Indian tribes, and likely several dozen more legitimate tribal nations that are not recognized. Some tribes are successful, others not so much, and many struggle mightily, tragically, to survive. The same is true within Indian tribes. There is the potential for much personal, petty jealousy and hate.

In American society, inequality reigns far more than within Indian country. The wealthiest 1 percent own almost all of the wealth of the world. Anger and jealousy and hate rule in American society. We see it every day in the news. The wealthiest, whether intentionally or not, have succeeded in turning the middle class and the poorest Americans against each other. Bear walk is everywhere. Not so in Indian country.

Perhaps because of monsters like bear walk, Anishinaabe Indian country has largely avoided the problem that dominates American society. No place or people is perfect, but tribal governments and Indian communities exist to help each other. We know what happens when society breaks down and communities turn on each other. We think about it all the time.

Bear walk surrounds Indian country. One writer in 2016 devoted an entire book to an attempt to tear apart Indian country. Naomi Schaefer Riley, a conservative journalist and political commentator published *The New Trail of Tears*, roundly denouncing all of federal Indian law and policy.[130] It could have been written in the nineteenth century, so full is it of stereotypes about Indian people and intentional misrepresentations of modern Indian tribes. Yet it is apparent it was written in the twenty-first century, with contemporaneous, up-to-date, racially charged signaling to an audience desperate for validation about white male supremacy. Schaefer Riley cynically seeks out Indian people themselves to make these misrepresentations and to restate these stereotypes. *New Trail* is an effort to turn Indian people on each other, a declaration of war against Indian people by white supremacists.

The trap for readers is that *New Trail* markets itself as a reform-minded book with deep sympathy for Indian people, with the federal government as the bad guy. Not so. At best, *New Trail* is paternalism, termination era– and allotment era–style illiberalism.[131] But that's too kind. Schaefer Riley characterizes the Indians that live in Indian country as poor, alcoholic, suicidal, shiftless rapists. She characterizes some Indians as really sad or frustrated people who are always slowly shaking their heads at the folly of other Indians. In short, Schaefer Riley detests Indian people.

New Trail's first sustained attack on Indian people is that all Indians want is a federal handout, which makes them behave like children. Schaefer Riley condemns the federal–tribal trust relationship as welfare that infantilized Indians: "Indeed, the trust authority has created a relationship whereby Indians will forever be treated as children, incapable of standing on their own feet."[132] *New Trail*, as an antigovernment screed, blames the United States for trying "to appease a crying toddler."[133] Her toddlers don't clean up their rooms, either, it appears. She delights in reporting that reservations she visited were dirty – claiming, for example, that the Crow Reservation is full of broken-down cars and trucks, broken windows, wrecked and dirty children's toys, lawn chairs, trash, and stray dogs.[134]

Schaefer Riley's racist labeling methods are careful. In most instances where *New Trail*'s text makes broad generalizations about the failings of Indian people, the most directly racist comments come from Indian people themselves, usually directed at other Indian tribes. One of her key sources on the Crow and Northern Cheyenne Reservations is Ivan Small, the director of the St. Labre Indian School, which made an $11 million payment to the Northern Cheyenne Tribe after being sued for "exploitation."[135] Small is quoted as criticizing Crow Reservation residents as not respecting the maxim, "A man's home is his castle."[136] He is the first of several Indian people in the book Schaefer Riley quotes as being angry at other Indians for a wide variety of character flaws. These informants are usually accusing Indians of flaws based on their status as Indian people – in other words, on their race. Schaefer Riley cynically quotes Indians to make these bigoted commentaries about Indians rather than quote overt racists. She often describes these Indians as slowly shaking their heads or muttering in frustration; Small is angry, but "mostly tired,"[137] and "past the point of anger."[138] Dobbs Oxendine from the Lumbee community is another of those Indians that was always slowly shaking his head, which Schaefer Riley says he did after he visited a reservation "out west."[139]

Schaefer Riley extends special appreciation to Ben Chavis, the controversial educator who is Lumbee. Chavis has a long history of

questionable financial dealings, leading to a 2017 federal court indictment,[140] as well as verbal abuse of students. He became famous for referring to some of his students as "darkies" and "half-breeds."[141] She
looks past Chavis's quite serious flaws to conclude that the man got
results: "One would be tempted to give a long leash to anyone [Cha-
vis] who could get such stellar academic results for students stuck in
America's worst performing districts."[142] In other words, the kind of
abuse Chavis heaped on his students, calling them by racial epithets
and humiliating them, was okay for Indian and poor students of color,
so long as they led to "results."

Schaefer Riley's celebration of Ben Chavis's racism extends to the
Lumbee Nation generally. Schaefer Riley begins her discussion of the
Lumbee Nation with Fergus Bordewich, who wrote a massively pop-
ular book in the 1990s titled *Killing the White Man's Indian*.[143] Elizabeth Cook-Lyn criticized that book for repeating falsely sympathetic
calls for reform of Indian affairs that would "further coloniz[e]" Indian people.[144] Schaefer Riley quotes Bordewich proposing that "Lumbees do not have any distinct racial characteristics."[145] Bordewich had
catalogued Indian people based on their racial characteristics and offered this take on the Lumbee people: "They run the physical gamut
from blond hair and blue eyes to the nearly Negroid[,]" no "memory,"
no "language," and they are "Baptist."[146] Weirdly, *New Trail* seems to
be making the case that Lumbees aren't Indians, and Schaefer Riley
says that's good, because for her being Indian is awful. Of course,
both Bordewich and Schaefer Riley were unaware of or don't care
that the Lumbees fought and won a literal war with the Ku Klux Klan
more than a half century ago, the Battle of Hayes Pond, establishing
and preserving a powerful identity of Indianness.[147] Schaefer Riley
obsesses over racial characteristics. She should have instead learned
about Indian people and their cultures.

Sadly, Schaefer Riley also employs quotes by Lumbee people
to attack other Indians; for example, quoting Cheryl Beasley saying
that "[the Rosebud Sioux Indians] just say to the federal government:
'Give us our check and tell us what to do.'"[148] Other nasty comments
come from Ben Chavis: "At one Oxendine stone just off the road,
it says, 'He was a quiet Indian leader who gave fiercely of his love,
time, counsel and wealth to others.' Chavis laughs: 'Translation: He

never had a job.'"[149] *New Trail* relies on Dobbs Oxendine to provide the standard antiwelfare commentaries about poor people of color: "Between food stamps and housing assistance, Oxendine believes no one has an incentive to work anymore."[150] And because no attack on Indian people is complete without invoking the drunken Indian stereotype,[151] *New Trail* includes one final Dobbs Oxendine line, this time in opposition to federal recognition of the Lumbee Nation: "If we get more checks, we will have more alcohol."[152]

But Schaefer Riley is not above making her own broad generalizations about the character of Indian people. In discussing American Indian parents, she condemns "most" Indians for not wanting their children to succeed:

> But there's also this: many of the parents don't want their kids to leave. It's almost the opposite of an immigrant mentality. If you spend enough time interviewing working-class parents who have recently come to America from the Dominican Republic or Mexico or Poland or Russia or Italy, you'll understand that as much as they love their children, they aren't hoping that as adults, their children won't move to a nicer neighborhood. For them, the whole point of coming to this country was to move up socially and economically. Most Native American parents don't share this attitude.[153]

Schaefer Riley apparently believes that Indian parents don't love their children as much as people from Dominican Republic or Mexico or Poland or Russia or Italy. This is unusually vituperative Indian-hating.

In the context of the Seneca Nation in New York, Schaefer Riley's attack on Indian people for being lazy and dependent on the government takes a surreal turn. The Seneca Nation is actually a quite wealthy tribe, with incredibly successful gaming operations. Before they got started in gaming in 2004, tribal members owned and operated smoke shops and gas stations in an incredibly dynamic and entrepreneurial economic environment. It is fair to say that Senecas are as entrepreneurial as anyone in the world. Schaefer Riley's attacks on other Indians for not being entrepreneurial doesn't work here, so *New Trail* accuses the Seneca Nation of being a haven for fascism.

Schaefer Riley's initial description of the Seneca Nation people is that they are rich in the wrong way. *New Trail* labels gaming revenue per capita payments "annuities," which was another way for the author to claim the Seneca Nation gets money from the government for nothing.[154] For Schaefer Riley, those "annuities," which derive from the nation's hard-earned gaming operations, stunts Seneca Indians' "entrepreneurial spirit."[155] *New Trail* caricatures Indian gaming as part of what she calls a "loophole economy," and not true entrepreneurship. Normally, economists refer to a "loophole economy" in the context of multinational corporations and wealthy individuals avoiding taxes through loopholes. But for Schaefer Riley, the loophole economy appears to be everything Indian tribes and Indian people have done for the past half century or more to generate revenue. She refuses to credit tribal economic activity as a product of entrepreneurial spirit, instead claiming tribal revenues are just accidental boondoggles that lazy Indians have stumbled upon. Billions of dollars are generated for tribal government purposes through gaming, smoke shops, gas stations, big box retail, federal contracting, sovereign lending, natural resources extraction, and so on. For Schaefer Riley, tribal economies do not result from entrepreneurial spirit but are instead mere coincidences arising from a "sovereign advantage."[156] I suspect she would have no problem with private corporate entities exploiting a loophole for financial gain, but she does have a problem with Indian tribes doing it.

In *New Trail's* telling, the Seneca Nation isn't successful at all. Schaefer Riley instead accuses the tribe of profiting from "a narrative of victimhood" and creating a "culture of dependency."[157] After reviewing her put-downs of the Seneca Nation, it is not clear to me how Indian people can ever be economically successful in a way that satisfies her extreme worldview.

New Trail's next attack on the Seneca Nation, and economically successful Indian nations more generally, is even more fanatical, and somehow involves a spirited defense of the nation of Israel. Schaefer Riley seems to be set off by the comparison a Seneca employee, David Kimelberg, makes to Israel of Senecas' efforts to stave off political destruction from states and the federal government: "People want to bomb you out of existence, and you need to make sure that doesn't happen."[158] Schaefer Riley either sees an opportunity to attack Senecas for being fascist, or is perhaps overreacting to the comparison of an Indian tribe to Israel, another politically powerful nation that depends in no small part on the United States. Schaefer Riley argues Israel is successful because of the strength of its people, but Seneca is successful because of a "top down" mentality, or central planning like China's: "You don't need to travel to Beijing to see central planning at work. It's everywhere on reservations."[159] Then she suggests that the Seneca Nation has turned itself into an authoritarian dictatorship with lots of cash: "Indeed, rather than turning into Israel, Senecas have created in upstate New York a kind of oil-rich sheikhdom like Saudi Arabia."[160] Schaefer Riley's attack on Seneca governance capacity and practices is that – no matter how successful – the tribal government is corrupt, like all tribal governments: "This is not to say that democracy doesn't exist in Seneca territory, but there are both a lot of patronage jobs to be had and a seemingly great deal of dissatisfaction among the members."[161] She blames the Seneca governance structure for political corruption, where "the president can't serve two consecutive terms" and political power is shared by the two reservations, Allegany and Cattaraugus.[162] Strangely, Schaefer Riley hates the Seneca Nation's notion of democracy because the tribe diffuses political power *too* much.

New Trail repeatedly accuses other tribal governments of corruption, too, but with little or no evidence. Schaefer Riley points to the Peter McDonald story of corruption at the Navajo Nation in the late 1970s as evidence of corruption in the twenty-first century, which was truly terrible at the time, but that's over now, and she grudgingly admits "matters have improved somewhat since then."[163] *New Trail* also alleges that the Crow Nation government is either corrupt or incompetent. There, Schaefer Riley quotes a tribal leader as saying that the Crow Nation owed $3 million to the Department of Housing and Urban Development and could not construct new housing until HUD was repaid. It turns out the tribe and HUD were deep in litigation, but in 2016, the year *New Trail* was published, HUD allocated $2.7 million to the tribe, so something must have been going right.

An enormous blind spot in *New Trail* is the agency that Indian people have exercised every day throughout the self-determination era, which began in force in the 1970s with the enactment of the Indian Self-Determination and Education Assistance Act (ISDEAA), also known as Public Law 638.[164] Under that law, more than 50 percent of federal government services provided to Indians and Indian tribes are administered by Indian tribes themselves as federal government contractors, and potentially someday it could be 100 percent. *New Trail*'s repetitive insistence that Indian people are lazy, dependent infants is belied by the reality that thousands upon thousands of Indian people work – and work damn hard – under self-determination contracts with the United States.

New Trail's only acknowledgment of the self-determination era is to quote William Allen, a Bush I–era Civil Rights Commission appointee: "After [ISDEAA], you began to get a steady stream of people coming back into the reservation, because it came with some pretty targeted federal funding."[165] This sounds like a good thing. But Schaefer Riley draws a negative conclusion: "Today it's the most vulnerable people who remain on the reservation. They're the ones with little education, little sense of what life outside the reservation might offer them, and little ambition."[166] So for Allen there was a steady stream of professional Indians going back home to administer self-determination contracts, but for Schaefer Riley the only Indians left in Indian country are ignorant and unmotivated.

Ian Haney López's *Dog Whistle Politics* details how Republican politicians following Barry Goldwater shifted their political rhetoric in the 1960s.[167] The strategy, called the Southern strategy, targeted poor and middle-class white voters by arguing that their problems were caused by people of color. More specifically, they argued that poor and middle-class whites paid the cost for the increases in federal appropriations for social services and other civil rights protections. Haney López shows how conservatives invented the myth of the welfare queen and the hyperviolent criminal to win over poor and middle-class whites. Instead of relying on direct racial confrontation and discrimination, conservatives created an entire new political language that equated government spending with lazy, shiftless, dependent brown-skinned people. Over time, the strategy worked. The southern region of the United States, and most rural areas, are now overwhelmingly Republican. Conservatives now dominate American politics with anti-tax rhetoric; case in point, the only major victory for the Republican Party during Trump's first year (2017) was a tax bill. Poor and middle-class whites too often believe the federal government exists to benefit people of color. The Southern strategy, one can plausibly argue, has been so successful that politicians can once again target with impunity people of color with the rhetoric of white supremacy.

New Trail is an effort to use that same dog-whistle political strategy to undermine the political will behind the federal tribal trust relationship. Schaefer Riley's descriptions of Indian people as dependent upon the federal government, who don't clean up their reservations, who aren't entrepreneurial come right from the dog-whistle political playbook. *New Trail*'s repetitive effort to label tribal governments as corrupt is an attack on governments generally. What the book doesn't do is document much of Schaefer Riley's allegations. Its evidence is a collection of anecdotes from shady characters like Ben Chavis who have extensive track records of improper conduct, coupled with Schaefer Riley's ideological commentaries on poor people of color. There is no evidence in *New Trail*. A dog whistle is intended to work without proof.

Schaefer Riley's work is a written form of the bear walk from Anishinaabe lore. *New Trail* is angry about the successes of Indian nations. It is jealous of the threat posed by the ideas arising in Indian country. Schaefer Riley wants Indian people to turn on each other with jealousy and hate. Schaefer Riley wants outsiders to turn on Indian people and Indian nations. Schaefer Riley is a bear walker. Don't let her into your home.

10

THE NON-INDIAN WAY OF LIFE

Anishinaabewaki is the word for the lands of the Anishinaabe, or even the world of the Anishinaabe. Anishinaabewaki is a vast homeland that includes the places where the ancestors are buried; the places where winter lodges, summer camps, and spring maple-sugaring camps are all located; and the places where the spirits roam. Anishinaabewaki is home to dozens upon dozens of Ojibwe, Odawa, and Bodewadmi Indian nations in Michigan, Wisconsin, Minnesota, and Ontario, Canada.

Eddie Benton-Benai's foundational work, *The Mishomis Book: The Voice of the Ojibwe* (1979), details the origins and the scope of Anishinaabewaki. The Anishinaabe originated at the mouth of what is now the St. Lawrence River and seaway. Thousands of years ago, the Anishinaabe migrated upriver to the western Great Lakes, where they nestled fitfully in between the Haudenosaunee and Sioux Nations. Anishinaabe storytellers described certain locations as way stations for the people, places like Manitoulin Island, Michilimackinac and Mackinac Island, Baweting (Sault Ste. Marie), Madeline Island – places that are still sacred to Anishinaabe people. Anishinaabe families established villages and farms close to these locations, spreading out over the land. Based on the season, Anishinaabe people moved around quite a bit, spending summers on the beach with their farms, hunting and fishing; wintering inland in small lodges with close family members; and spending spring at the maple-sugaring locations, before returning to the beaches in summer.

The Anishinaabe also established a governance system based on a clan system. Loon and crane clans typically were the leadership clans. The turtle or fish clan served as the speakers and intellectuals, and resolved disputes between the leadership and other clans. The marten and bear clans were the muscle, the martens serving as warriors and the bears as the peacekeepers. The deer and the bird clans were more spiritual and gentle clans.

The coming of the non-Indians disrupted many Anishinaabe traditions. The disruption often came with violence and famine. Certain Anishinaabe people with particular strengths and skills rose to become *ogemaag* (leaders), tasked by their communities to lead war parties, to speak at treaty negotiations, or to lead tribal communities through difficult periods of starvation and disease. Over time, relying on the strengths and advantages of the Anishinaabeg, most Anishinaabe communities were able to negotiate complete agreements with the United States and Canada that preserved at least a small part of Anishinaabewaki for their exclusive homelands.

The post-treaty story of the Michigan Odawa nations in northwest lower Michigan is not a pretty one.[168] The United States completely failed to properly implement and administer its obligations to the Odawa nations. The government did not survey or establish the reservations. The government did not properly respect the property rights established in the treaties for either the tribes or the individual Indians. The government even refused to deal with the tribes, an illegal act now referred to as administrative termination. Because the trust relationship broke down between the Odawa nations and the United States, those tribes lost almost all the lands intended for their reservations through fraud, coercion and violence, and corruption.

In the 1980s and 1990s, the United States had restored federal recognition of three Michigan Odawa Indian nations. By then, the tribal land base was sparse. Many tribal citizens had dispersed to the cities, often pushed by the Bureau of Indian Affairs, for education and jobs. And non-Indians lived on lands once claimed by the grandparents and great-grandparents of Odawa people. Anishinaabe people had specific and deeply emotional memories of ancestors who lost their lands. One Odawa man described how deceitful non-Indians defrauded his community of land near the Little River Band of Ottawa Indians Reservation:

> One Ottawa man said, "I was born at Stoney Lake, in Benona Township, west of Shelby in Oceana County, in 1903. There's a place on the south side of [the lake] that belongs to all t[he] Indians at one time." A man named Porter, who realized the value of this lake-front property for summer resorts, called a meeting of the Indian property owners. He claimed to be a government agent, and offered to act as their agent to sell the property for a tremendous amount of money. A Miss "Korski" and a Doctor "Rosin" who worked at the girls' summer camp in the area persuaded the Indians to sign papers which, they said, gave Porter the right to sell the property for them. Each Indian was asked to contribute cash to cover sale expenses. The people actually signed quit-claim deeds and Porter stamped them with a government seal which he had stolen, to make the deal look official, took their money without providing receipts, and left. "Well, he sold it, then he kept the money. Nobody prosecute him or nothing. Now what the hell you gonna do in those days?"[169]

Emmet County, where the Waganakising Odawa Nation is located, is a rural resort community. An informal, but real caste system is in place there. Emmet and neighboring Charlevoix County is Ernest Hemingway country. As a child, Ernest Hemingway summered on Walloon Lake and environs near Petoskey, Michigan. Some of his earliest writings involve Indian people there. His experience as a wealthy outsider enjoying the beautiful summertime environment is prototypical. Thousands of outsiders, many of whom are incredibly affluent, visit there regularly. These outsiders own much of the best land near the shore, and they bring in the business that keeps the local community economically viable. These summer people constitute the top caste. The second caste might be called the locals. They live there year-round and provide services to the summer people. Steve Amick's novel, *The Lake, the River, and the Other Lake* (2005), based on his own experiences summering on the northern Michigan shorelines, nicely describes the love-hate relationship between summer people and locals – locals live there year-round and do all the work, but everything is dominated by the summer people, who seem to own all the good land and control the bulk of the money and resources.

Both the summer people and the locals have even more in common – they are not Indians. The Waganakising Odawa, and other Indian people, are in the bottom caste. Historically, they were the poorest of the poor, their homes improperly weatherized, their employment mostly dangerous manual labor, and their kids taken to Holy Childhood boarding school, often against their will. Bill Dunlop's memoir, *The Indians of Hungry Hollow* (2004), details growing up Odawa in Petoskey in the first half of the twentieth century. Even now they struggle, surrounded by the trappings of incredible wealth. Mixed in the community with wealthy and poor white people, Odawa people have long been in dire straits. The summer people and the locals too often join together to oppose the tribe's efforts to save the environment, or develop economic ventures, or assert influence over school boards, zoning commissions – everything. It is Cheryl Harris's philosophy, Whiteness as Property,[170] writ large.

Recently, one of those Odawa nations, the Little Traverse Bay Bands of Odawa Indians, also known as the Waganakising Odawa, filed suit against the state of Michigan, Emmet County, and other state entities.[171] The tribe is seeking a specific form of relief that would bar state and local officials from asserting jurisdiction over tribal citizens and the tribe within the reservation boundaries promised by the United States in the 1836 and 1855 treaties.[172] The key impact for tribal members would be that Indian child welfare matters arising in state court would have to be transferred to tribal court, certain crimes committed by tribal members would be transferred to tribal court, and tribal immunities from state and local taxation and regulations would be enhanced.

The top caste, the wealthy property owners, and to some extent the middle caste, are terrified and outraged. The Emmet County Lakeshore Association formed an entity called the Protection of Rights Alliance Foundation and began raising money to fight the tribe. They retained a prominent Lansing, Michigan, law firm steeped in state Republican Party politics to participate in the litigation and help to organize a political response. The property owners' response epitomizes modern Indian-hating.

The lakeshore association distributed a summary of the lawsuit in summer 2016 detailing its Indian-hating.[173] The summary attempts to bind together non-Indians to protect the "Northern Michigan way of life," a decidedly non-Indian way of life. The association's additional stated purposes are to "promote the health, welfare and safety of the community" and "protect and preserve the natural beauty and environment" on the Emmet County shoreline. Emmet County is characterized by its fabulous and exclusive resorts, offering, among other things, skiing in the winter and water sports in the summer. There are thriving, upscale clothing stores and five-star restaurants. The lakeshores, both inland lakes and on Lake Michigan itself, are dominated by private condominiums and mansions. There are thousands of high-end rental properties for the summer people. Emmet County is wine country, too, and there is a growing organic farming community.

The lakeshore association's summary declares, however, that if the tribe prevails in the suit, "important rights and protections that non-Indians have enjoyed in the past will abruptly end, and the land and lifestyles that non-Indians pass on to the next generation will be fundamentally diminished." Helpfully, the summary details what will happen to Emmet County a decade after it is declared "Indian country"[174] by a federal court. Property values will have "plummeted" so much that an Indian person would be able to afford a lakeshore home in Emmet County. "A lakeside homeowner on [state highway] M-119 will find that the adjacent property has been bought by a member of the Tribe with plans to redevelop the property as a convenience store with a flea market during summer months." "There will be several fast food restaurants in both downtown Petoskey and downtown Harbor Springs," the two major towns in the county. Most gas stations and convenience stores will become mini-casinos with slot machines. "There will be a host of wind farms in the region, several located along the shoreline where the winds are the heaviest and most consistent."

Flea markets. Fast food restaurants. Slot machines. Wind farms.

Apparently, these are the commercial and energy activities that are antithetical to the northern Michigan resort rural way of life. But it is apparent that the lakeshore association's leaders and advisors also believe Indian people are lower class, confirming the informal caste system Indians have known about all their lives. For the association, it seems, Indian business interests are uncomplicated and unambitious – selling cheap goods and trash entertainment. Putting Indians in charge would transform the pristine northern way of life into a series of shoddy strip malls at best and a desolate ghetto of poverty and crime dominated by people with brown skins. And all of that presumably powered by wind energy infrastructure.

For the lakeshore association, these horrors will be enabled by two critical changes to Emmet County that would naturally follow from the tribe's victory in federal court. First, tribal governance would dominate over local governments and the state. Local zoning that limits or even prevents fast food restaurants from springing up in downtown Harbor Springs and precludes private property owners from turning their lakefront homes into swap meets would be preempted by permissive tribal zoning. Worse for the landowners, the hated federal government, which has jurisdiction over Indian country, could enable the tribe to enforce its more protective and restrictive environmental regulations in Emmet County, undoing commercial development proposals – at least the ones favored by the lakeshore association's members. Non-Indians could be hauled into tribal court to answer for their torts and contract breaches, and perhaps even to resolve property disputes.

Second, for lakeshore association members, tribal governance likely would depress property values. Longtime Emmet County residents who depend on a robust real estate market, summer people primarily, believe that a tribal victory in federal court would discourage buyers and renters from entering Emmet County, who would then go elsewhere. And don't forget all the low-class commercial activities like swap meets and fast food restaurants that the Indians would bring to the shores and the downtown areas.

Of course, none of these allegations are likely to occur, or make much of a difference. The tribe isn't asking for – and could never receive from any federal court – an order completely superseding state and local government. Federal law protects non-Indians from Indian tribes, limiting tribal civil jurisdiction over non-Indian lands unless the non-Indian expressly consents to tribal jurisdiction. That kind of consent involves a tribe's business partners and employees, casino patrons, and very few others. The lakeshore association's law firm, which has extensive experience in this area, is ethically obligated to explain the limits of tribal jurisdiction over non-Indians. Either there is a significant miscommunication between the lakeshore association and its lawyers, the lakeshore association is ignoring its lawyers, or perhaps the lawyers are unethically enabling the lakeshore's statements about the law. It wouldn't be the first time lawyers enabled unethical behavior in Indian country.

What's missing from all this, too, is that the tribe has just as much of an interest in maintaining the veneer of wealth and class as the summer people and the locals do. The tribe operates casino resorts in the area and would lose everything if the summer people and the locals stopped patronizing the tribe's properties.

The real disconnect here is between the lakeshore association's views on government and the tribe's values. The current dominant government structure in Emmet County enables an economic structure that favors the wealthy summer people and, to a much lesser extent, the lower-middle-class locals. The summer people, who probably do not vote in great numbers in local elections, still dominate local politics through the promise of cash spent in the county. Summer people presumably pay vast sums in property taxes as well. The locals who serve the summer people, and who elect the local governments that preserve the current governance structure, are effectively under the thumb of the summer people and the promise of summer money.

The tribe worries that Odawa citizens receive short shrift in local governance. The tribe complains that local courts refuse to transfer Indian child welfare matters to the tribal court under the Indian Child

Welfare Act.[175] Tribal citizen children, and their parents, stand to receive more attention and better services from the tribe than from the state. The tribe doesn't routinely seek to terminate the parental rights of its citizens except in cases of criminal abuse, and has adopted a culturally appropriate adoption program. The tribe further complains that tribal citizens arrested as juveniles and for nonviolent first-time offenses are punished severely under state law. In tribal court, tribal citizens arrested for nonviolent drug offenses or alcohol-related status offenses could be diverted into the tribal court's Waabshki-Miigwan Drug Court Program that provides culturally sensitive services. The program has had enormous success in its first decade. In state court, all the tribal citizens receive is a criminal record and random drug tests.

The tribe has also long complained that the state and local governments benefit disproportionately from the tribe's governmental and business enterprises. Under its gaming compact, the tribe already pays local units of government 2 percent of its profits, an amount that overcompensates the county for lost taxes and other costs it incurs arising from the casino operations. The tribe has built millions of dollars' worth of government buildings on trust land, where state and local taxes are not supposed to be imposed, but the state has imposed those taxes off-reservation on the tribe's contractors, which pass the costs down to the tribe. From the tribe's perspective, the state and local governments receive a windfall from the tribe's business operations.

Empirical truth or falsity of the lakeshore association's worries aside, the dispute appears to be more about the philosophies of the property owners versus the tribe and its citizens, "the northern Michigan way of life." The lakeshore association wants to maintain its privileged position allowing summer residents to enjoy Emmet County's scenery, entertainments, and protections – to disrupt nothing. The tribe's complaints are not against the lakeshore association or any property owners, despite the fact that twenty-first century non-Indian property owners directly benefit from illegal acts taken against Odawa people.

Regardless of the ultimate outcome of the Little Traverse Odawa lawsuit, the Anishinaabeg will continue to govern in a manner consistent with the tribe's traditions, rooted in Mino-Bimaadiziwin.

THE NON-INDIAN WAY OF LIFE   103

From that view, all Anishinaabe Inaakonigewin (law) derives. From Mino-bimaadziwin, we learn the Seven Grandmother (or Grandfather) teachings: Nibwaakaawin – Wisdom; Zaagidwin – Love; Manaadjitowaawin – Respect; Aakodewin – Bravery; Gwekowaadiziwin – Honesty; Dibaadenizowin – Humility; and Debwewin – Truth (see pp. xvi–xvii). These are principles of fundamental fairness and justice. Imagine a local government, say a county commission or school board, adopting these principles in their foundational documents and charters. American government is about power, but not about justice.

Waganakising Odawa tribal governance can no longer depend so heavily on the ancient and traditional manner of government through the clan system, but the underlying philosophy of that structure is intact. Now, tribal leaders are selected through American-style elections, a product of federal intervention and the tribe's acquiescence to certain forms of nontribal political philosophies. But tribal elections at Waganakising are not controlled or even influenced by outsiders. Elected officials are not proxies for monied interests; they do not kowtow to the summer people. They take the Seven Grandmother (or Grandfather) teachings seriously. They take Mino-bimaadziwin seriously. They respect the interests of the summer people and the locals, and recognize that the interests of the Waganakising Odawa are often the same as those of the rest of Emmet County.

From its writings, it seems apparent that the lakeshore association and its counsel see every interaction with the Waganakising Odawa as a zero-sum game. If the tribe wins, the property owners lose. The tribe sees things in a different way, a way in which everyone wins if the tribe wins.

11

THE *MARTINEZ* FIXERS

There is a new story floating around Anishinaabewaki (the world of the Anishinaabeg) attributed to a Michigan Anishinaabe *inini* (man).[176] He tells the story of a pack of wolves. They work together. They hunt and sleep together. They defend a territory. They do what wolves do, and it works for them. One day in the early spring, maybe Onaabani-giizis (Hard Crust on the Snow Moon, or March), when food is scarce, a young *mai'ingan* (wolf) sniffs something different across the lake. His pack is moving on, so he doesn't linger long, but he does linger. The next time out, *mai'ingan* smells the smell again, and it smells good. He's even hungrier this time. His pack moves on, but he lingers and then breaks off from the pack. He investigates the smell. Across the lake, a human family has constructed a lodge. They're cooking. And it smells extremely delicious to the young *mai'ingan*. He hesitates for a long while, but his hunger overcomes his reluctance, and he travels over the still-frozen lake to the lodge. The humans are delighted to see *mai'ingan*. They're new to the area and don't realize their new neighbor is a wolf. They throw scraps of their delicious, bountiful food to the young *mai'ingan*, who eats greedily. These new people call him "dog" because they don't know any better.

The young *mai'ingan* begins to return to the lodge again and again, until one day he doesn't return to his pack at all. He stays at the lodge all the time, eating the food the humans in the lodge set out for him. He forgets about his life with the pack. After a time, the humans become less interested in the young *mai'ingan*. They don't always remember to toss him

scraps. The wolf becomes hungry again. And he becomes thin, emaciated, mangy. The humans eventually scorn the young *mai'ingan*. He is no
longer welcome. He leaves the lodge and wanders, not sure what to do.
He looks terrible. He sees other wolves, wolves from his old pack, but he
doesn't recognize them and they don't recognize him. As he wanders,
some things become familiar again; he begins to remember where he
came from, who he was close to, his pack. And they begin to remember
him. Eventually, the young *mai'ingan* returns to his pack, his family. The
message is that Indian people have to try to remember who they are, who
their relatives are, and what they can do to make their relatives and their
ancestors proud.

There are a lot of problems with Indian country governance. Indian-hating in the form of colonialism has a done a number on tribal cultures. But things have turned around for tribal nations since the 1970s
when Congress made possible modern tribal self-determination, starting with Public Law 638.[177] Yet the legal and governmental structures
that Indian people now manage are still edifices of colonialism. They
are governments established for Indian people by non-Indian people.
And they create non-Indian problems for Indian people to solve.

Indian people have always attempted to resolve internal tribal political disputes internally. Vine Deloria, Jr. once wrote that traditional
tribal governance structures usually were reactive entities that served
as a kind of protojudiciary, meaning that tribal councils typically met
to resolve internal disputes.[178] Anishinaabe nations traditionally relied
upon collective decision-making in order to address internal problems. These internal problems could range from intrafamily squab-
bles to political intrigue to violent crimes. The council might consist
of elders, respected community members appointed by consensus,
ogemaag (leaders), a completely original group, or a combination of
any of the above. Whatever the entity or whomever the group of people, dispute resolution came from within.

As the United States gradually gained power and status over Indian nations in the nineteenth century, the federal government began to routinely interfere in internal tribal political issues. From the

mid-nineteenth century to the 1880s, federal officials used the power to distribute resources (food, money, clothing, and so on) to reservation Indians to influence and often control reservation affairs. Indian agents and reservation superintendents used their power to select tribal leaders, favor Indian people who supported federal policies, and undermine tribal cultures and language. In the 1880s, the US Supreme Court broadly confirmed the plenary power of Congress over Indian affairs, including internal tribal political matters.[179] Congress and federal Indian affairs officials took advantage of this power from that point until the 1930s, when the Department of the Interior's own studies concluded that various federal initiatives had been terrific failures for Indian people and Indian nations.[180] By that time, though, the United States had disestablished the powerful tribal governments of the so-called Five Civilized Tribes in Oklahoma; established federally controlled governments at Navajo, Hopi, and other resource-rich Indian nations; and dominated reservation politics throughout Indian country. The Indian Reorganization Act of 1934 established federal rules allowing Indian nations to reestablish tribal control over reservation affairs.[181] World War II and termination era of the 1950s intervened and stunted tribal political growth. The act's promise went unfulfilled, largely, until the establishment of the self-determination era of the 1970s, which continues today.

Attempting to continue some form of federal dominance over internal tribal affairs, Congress enacted the Indian Civil Rights Act (ICRA) in 1968.[182] ICRA was a passion project of Senator Sam Ervin, a white southern segregationist. His secretary, the story goes, was Lumbee. Ervin supposedly contrasted his secretary, who by all accounts was a successful professional working in Congress, to the stories he heard of Indians who were struggling throughout Indian country in the early 1960s. Ervin decided that the best thing for reservation Indians was to impose federal civil rights law on them, Indian-hating by paternalism and good intentions. By then, some Indian tribes had established nascent tribal governments controlled by Indian people. The lack of consistently applied standards, either borrowed from American government structures or reestablished tribal governance models, undermined the efficacy of those early modern tribal governments. A few federal cases holding that the US Constitution

did not restrict tribal government actions suggested to critics of tribal governments, and advocates of individual Indian civil rights, that
tribal governments were lawless. Congress intended the 1968 act to
bring law to these Indians.

In the first decade after ICRA's passage, no one really knew how
to enforce it. Most civil rights advocates, including the US Department of Justice and reservation legal services providers, proceeded as
if the federal courts were the proper place to enforce ICRA. Federal
courts began hearing due process and equal protection challenges to
tribal elections, tribal political processes, and tribal citizenship decisions. Some federal courts agreed that ICRA created federal rights
that should be enforceable in federal courts, but other federal courts
dismissed those claims as improperly interfering with tribal sovereignty. If ICRA was enforceable in federal courts, and those federal
courts applied federal constitutional legal principles to tribal governments, ICRA would have replaced tribal legal principles completely.
Indian tribes would be subject to federal law on all questions of internal tribal governance, from elections to membership to property laws
to zoning laws. ICRA would have been, perhaps, the most invasive
form of federal intervention in tribal government, Indian-hating writ
large, whether intentional or not.

Eventually, the US Supreme Court concluded in *Santa Clara
Pueblo v. Martinez* that tribal forums were the proper, and only, place
to enforce ICRA's civil rights protections.[183] There, a citizen of the
Santa Clara Pueblo in northern New Mexico challenged a tribal membership ordinance that gave preferential treatment to the children of
tribal member men and not tribal member women. Justice Thurgood
Marshall's opinion sided with tribal interests to conclude that civil
rights claims must be brought in tribal forums. There, tribal courts or
other decision makers could interpret ICRA's Anglo American–style
guarantees of due process and equal protection in light of tribal customs and traditions.

Much of Indian country rejoiced at the decision as an enormous
victory for tribal sovereignty. But as Catharine MacKinnon pointed
out, the victory came at the expense of an Indian woman and her
children.[184] The Supreme Court's decision took power away from the
federal courts but vested that power in tribal governments that might

or might not be fair to persons under tribal jurisdiction. However, tribal governments had adopted American-style justice systems, retained American law–trained lawyers to draft tribal constitutions and codes as positive tribal law, and appointed American law–trained judges to interpret those laws. As a practical matter, that meant tribal interpretations of the due process and equal protections in ICRA closely followed federal interpretations under the US Constitution. I conducted a study in 2008 with a law student named Alicia Ivory (now Archer) looking at tribal court decisions published in the *Indian Law Reporter*, the leading tribal court reporter from the 1980s to the 2000s.[185] We found that in virtually all the decisions interpreting ICRA, the courts relied on federal jurisprudence. In all cases involving nonmember defendants, tribal courts *always* followed federal precedents. One might agree or disagree with the outcomes in those cases, but the decisions were wholly consistent with the scope of decisions made by federal and state courts.

No human-crafted constitution is perfect. Just as there are abuses of civil rights countenanced by federal and state governments, there are abuses by tribal governments as well. In recent decades, intractable tribal political disputes – almost always arising within tribal governments operating successful gaming operations – have arisen. These disputes usually involve an election dispute and a related effort to remove or banish certain tribal citizens, a process known as disenrollment. At any given time, as many as ten to twenty Indian nations might be going through an intractable dispute. In some instances, as with the Cherokee Nation and the Ho-Chunk Nation in the 1990s, and the Sac and Fox Nation of Iowa in the 2000s, the tribal government can no longer function for a time. At that point, one might think the federal government would step in to restore order. But no. The government has followed the principles of the *Martinez* decision deferring to tribal sovereignty and stays out of internal tribal disputes. The government might hold up federal appropriations to a tribe where it cannot determine conclusively which faction has legitimate control of a tribe, but this is an unusually rare occurrence. And when it does happen, and tribal government services start to shut down, the tribe quickly comes together to resolve the dispute. It's a lot like federal shutdowns that occur when Congress cannot reach a budget decision. These internal tribal political disputes are usually resolved fairly quickly and conclusively in tribal justice systems.

On rare occasions, as with the Nooksack Indian Tribe in the Pacific Northwest, the Saginaw Chippewa Indian Tribe of Michigan, and several other small tribes with no tribal courts, majority tribal political groups have moved to disenroll minority tribal members regardless of civil rights protections. These abuses are sparking a backlash against tribal governments generally, not just the tribes who are bad actors. News commentators, political actors, and even state and federal judges routinely make statements critical of tribes when they argue outsiders should stay out of internal tribal politics.[186]

For the first time, there appears to be a concerted effort by Indian lawyers and Indian law scholars to advocate for repealing or overturning *Martinez*. One legal scholar, Andrea Seielstad, previously a strong advocate for tribal sovereign immunity, now argues that without federal judicial review of ICRA claims, tribal governmental civil rights abuses will worsen.[187] Whether a congressional fix is viable as a political matter is almost impossible to determine at this writing, but when Indian affairs legislation happens, it often slips in under the radar at Congress. That usually means nothing will happen, but on occasion, as with the 2013 Violence against Women Reauthorization Act,[188] enormous changes can happen quickly, even unexpectedly.

As for a Supreme Court decision overturning *Martinez*? Well, that seems extremely unlikely given that the court has not agreed to review an ICRA-based civil rights claim, or any tribal member civil rights claim against a tribe since *Martinez* itself. Moreover, the rule adopted in *Martinez* follows a cherished conservative doctrinal policy of not opening up the federal courthouse doors to civil rights complainants.

However, a powerful conservative advocacy organization, the Goldwater Institute, has jumped on the backlash against *Martinez* in order to undermine the Indian Child Welfare Act of 1978 (ICWA).[189] Goldwater's broad claims against ICWA involve constitutional challenges to the power of Congress.[190] But their claims are blunted severely by the reality that outcomes for Indian children in cases where the courts comply with ICWA are far better than outcomes in state court. Goldwater's gambit here is to attack tribal justice systems and tribal laws as abusive, citing the problems of disenrollment. Goldwater's weakness on this front requires them to hope their audience ignores the twin logical fallacies here that not all tribes are the same, and that internal political disputes are not the same as Indian child welfare decisions made by state and tribal courts. Goldwater's attack on *Martinez* suffers from the same practical problems as the previous challenges. Congress probably won't do anything about it, and the Supreme Court has no reason to overrule its decision in *Martinez*.

For the sake of argument, let's address outcomes if *Martinez* is overruled by legislation or court order. Consider an election dispute arising at the Grand Traverse Band of Ottawa and Chippewa Indians. A few years back, I wrote an opinion for the tribal judiciary dismissing a challenge to an election board decision, *Raphael v. Election Board*.[191] The matter involved a recall petition against a sitting elected official. We dismissed the petition because we concluded the tribal judiciary did not have jurisdiction. The petitioner argued that if the tribal court did not have jurisdiction, her due process rights would be violated. She cited to the provision in the tribal constitution guaranteeing due process, a provision borrowed from the Indian Civil Rights Act.[192] At Grand Traverse Band, we interpret due process challenges in election disputes in accordance with the Seven Grandfather (or Grandmother) Teachings, Niizhwaaswi Mishomis Kinoomaageminowaan (see pp. xvi–xvii). The teachings are Nibwaakaawin (Wisdom), Zaagidwin (Love), Manaadjitowaawin (Respect), Aakodewin (Bravery), Gwekowaadiziwin (Honesty), Dibaadenizowin (Humility), and Debwewin (Truth). Although we worried about the election board's actions, we found no constitutional authority to review their decisions in the recall context.

Assuming *Martinez* was "fixed," the petitioner could have brought a federal district court action under the Indian Civil Rights Act to review our decision. Perhaps the legislation or court decision opening the courthouse doors would make clear whether federal or tribal laws would govern a federal claim under ICRA, but let's assume the federal court would apply tribal laws. The federal court could conclude, after reviewing the Seven Grandfather (or Grandmother) teachings, that the tribal judiciary was wrong to dismiss the challenge to the election board's recall petition matter. Surely that would be a fascinating opinion for a federal judge to craft!

Or let's assume federal laws could control the ICRA due process claim. The tribal judiciary's precedents concerning the Seven Grandfather (or Grandmother) teachings would be irrelevant, as would the election board's rules promising to comply with the Seven Grandfathers. The election board's rules, generated to govern an election involving perhaps one thousand or so tribal members (there are approximately four thousand members, but only about a quarter of them vote in a given election), might not be in compliance with federal constitutional mandates. It's hard to imagine how the Seven Grandfathers (or Grandmothers) and federal due process jurisprudence could coexist in the same universe, even where the outcomes of applying both sets of rules might be largely the same. Most importantly, a federal court could easily conclude that the tribal constitutional provision barring appeals from election board decisions is an unconstitutional denial of a right to appeal – a right to appeal articulated and announced by the federal court itself. Tribal member appeals from tribal election board might as well go straight to the federal district court in Grand Rapids or Kalamazoo. What an odd result! Federal courts would control tribal governance through the ICRA. Again, Indian-hating writ large.

To be fair, there are intractable political disputes arising from difficult election matters that tribal and nontribal parties create and profit from by exploiting the *Martinez* decision and related federal policies. At any given moment, ten to twenty-five Indian nations might be governed by a so-called holdover council. A holdover council situation arises when the majority of duly elected tribal council members refuse to vacate office after an election they lost. The losing candidates usually claim the election was irreparably flawed. Or they might not, and simply refuse to leave office. Several mechanisms kick into play at that moment. The first is tribal administrative or judicial review of the decision by the holdover council members to stay. For most tribes with holdover councils, there is no functioning tribal judiciary, rendering any tribal review irrelevant. But if there is a judiciary, challengers to the holdover council may begin proceedings there. Those proceedings take time and legal resources, which are not cheap. And when the tribal court proceedings are finally concluded, the tribal court might issue an order against the holdover council, an order the holdover council will most certainly ignore. The holdover council might even try to remove the tribal judiciary. The holdover council members already rejected an election outcome by hundreds or thousands of voters; a tribal court order from a few judges would be no different.

The next step is to the Bureau of Indian Affairs (BIA), usually a regional superintendent or director. There, the challengers to the holdover council would ask the BIA for a decision that the election was valid, forcing the removal of the holdover council members. *Martinez* on its face was limited to tribal civil rights issues, but the decision also reaffirmed that Indian nations had exclusive jurisdiction over internal affairs such as tribal citizenship and elections. *Martinez* marked a time when the Department of the Interior began stepping away from overseeing tribal governments. That federal deference to tribal sovereignty likely would compel the BIA superintendent or director to decide the BIA had no jurisdiction to intervene, and decline to make a decision on the election challenge. However, some tribal constitutions do allow for federal review, which could grant the BIA jurisdiction to decide the election matter. But those constitutions are pretty rare. More likely, the BIA officer will have to decide at some point which tribal government faction (the holdover council or the group that prevailed in the election) to recognize as the proper entity eligible to receive services and self-determination funding from the United States. Eventually, the BIA superintendent or director will issue a letter ruling of some sort.

None of that really matters because whichever side not favored by the letter will appeal the decision to the Interior Board of Indian Appeals (IBIA). If the holdover council is asked to set down, it will appeal. If the group that prevailed in the election is not satisfied with the BIA letter, they will appeal. The IBIA rightfully applies the strong federal policy favoring tribal resolution of internal tribal matters. Most times, especially if a significant amount of time has passed between the last election and the next election, the IBIA will slow its decision-making process down, or stop it altogether, to wait for the next election. That way the IBIA doesn't have to interfere with the internal tribal political process. It also means the holdover council prevails, and in some cases having effectively stolen an entire term. For the worst actors, the process begins anew with the next tribal election. Certain tribal leaders and attorneys know this system well. They play it brilliantly. Their opponents begin to curse the *Martinez* decision and think about ways to break down this cycle, about ways to force federal court review of tribal election decisions. Apparently, these advocates believe a federal court order requiring holdover council members to leave office will work when a tribal court order would not. Federal officers once dominated reservation affairs, choosing elected leaders and favoring certain families over others. Reintroducing federal officials into internal tribal politics comes with risks. Imagine a Trump administration judicial or Interior Department appointee influencing, and acting as the final arbiter, of a tribe's political decisions. Perhaps federal intervention will work for those tribes with truly intractable political disputes. Perhaps not.

Still, a one-size-fits-all *Martinez* fix would be a huge negative for tribes that have few, or only simple, election disputes. Tribes like Grand Traverse Band are just beginning to explore what modern tribal governance looks like when merged with or influenced by traditional decision-making philosophies. Congress designed ICRA to do just that, way back when Indian-hater Senator Sam Ervin championed assimilation through federal civil rights in the 1960s. It would be so sad to see nascent tribal governance short-circuited again. Tribal governments are learning to rediscover their traditions, like the *mai'ingan* that went away to live with people and then came back to his pack. It's a painful process, no doubt, but a worthy one.

12

EQUAL RIGHTS ÜBER ALLES

Anishinaabe people know of the story of the deserted boy.[193] There once was a boy who was the son of the *ogema* (leader) in the village. He was a much loved and much spoiled child. One day, the boy killed his playmates. The village must have been devastated. But this boy was just a child. The *ogema* instructed the child never to kill another child again, or else the entire village would desert the child, leaving him to live out the rest of his days alone. Some time passed, and the child killed another child. The *ogema* deserted the child. He moved the village away, and instructed the child to stay. He became the deserted boy.

More time passed. A boy named Taimisi who had known the deserted boy wondered how he was doing, alone there in the old village. Taimisi took a few of his friends and went to visit the deserted boy. They found the deserted boy thriving in the old village. The *manidowaag* (spirits) had blessed him. Taimisi and his friends played stick games with the deserted boy, and before long the deserted boy had won from them all their treasures. Taimisi and his friends left, but before long, they decided to return to gamble with the deserted boy again in order to win back their treasures. So they did. And they beat the deserted boy playing the moccasin game (a game where an object is hidden in a group of moccasins, and the player has to guess where it is). They won everything they had lost. They won all of the deserted boy's treasures. They even won the deserted boy's lodge. Now, the deserted boy's lodge was made of stone, so Taimisi and his friends couldn't take it back home with them. Instead, they decided to stay the night and make the deserted boy tell stories. And so they did. The deserted boy told stories inside the stone lodge. One by one, Taimisi's friends fell asleep. Taimisi struggled to keep them awake, but he failed. Eventually, even Taimisi fell asleep. When he awoke a short time later, the deserted boy was gone. But the entrance to the lodge was in flames. Soon, the entire lodge would burn with Taimisi and all his friends inside. Taimisi was able to rouse his friends and escape. They were able to save some of the treasures inside. On their way out of the village, they saw the deserted boy, who called out, "There goes Taimisi who caused me to lose my home! He burned my lodge with fire!"

Taimisi shook his head, bewildered by the deserted boy's behavior. "He who set fire to his own home knows not what he is saying!" Taimisi looked around at his friends. Some of them carried many items they had rescued from the burning lodge. But most of them carried few or no items. The stated moral of this story is that few Anishinaabe would ever acquire much wealth.

There is more to learn from this story. The deserted boy is an enigma. From a tragically young age, he is a relentless killer. He kills children again and again. He drives his family and his people away. He is left alone, deserted. But even as a deserted boy, somehow he acquires great wealth, and his wealth attracts others to him. He tries to kill them, too, and burns down his own home. In the end, the deserted boy is still alone. He has lost his home and his possessions. And he is left blaming others for his troubles.

The Citizens Equal Rights Foundation (CERF), closely allied with the Citizens Equal Rights Alliance (CERA), is one of the more active anti-Indian hate groups in America, according to the Institute for Research and Education on Human Rights. The group also affiliates with the Upstate Citizens for Equality group, and the Central New York Fair Business Association. The principals in CERF/CERA travel around the country to areas where white supremacists live close to Indian country, agitating against Indian people, tribal nations, and the federal government. They focus their hate on Indians. They see Indians and tribes advocate for treaty rights. They see tribes purchase land and put up health clinics, gas stations, cop shops, casino resorts, and tribal justice centers, while the non-Indian governments provide less and non-Indian businesses pay less or go out of business. They hate Indians. They blame Indians for unemployment, mortgage fore-closures, cancer. As Megan McCune shows, however, local support for these groups dissipates as soon as an Indian tribe begins hiring locals at the tribe or its enterprises.[194] Witness the dramatic political turnaround when Madison and Oneida Counties supported the Oneida Indian Nation's omnibus settlement agreement to end its various law-suits with the state of New York several years ago.

The Indian-hating principals who travel around to agitate also file a lot of amicus briefs in federal court (amicus briefs are filed by "friends of the court," people or entities that file additional briefs to provide greater context to the court in important cases). These amicus briefs are unhinged. Consider the one filed by James J. Devine, Jr. for CERF in *Washington v. United States*, which claims a massive conspiracy theory linking James Madison, Richard Nixon, Barack Obama, federal government lawyers, and Indian tribes in a plot to overthrow the United States.[195] The case is about whether Indian trea-ty rights protect salmon habitat in the Pacific Northwest, so one might wonder how we get from there to the end of America.

Initially, I'll try to summarize the factual predicates for CERF's conspiracy, none of which are all that controversial. First, the US Supreme Court acknowledged its jurisdiction to enjoin violations of Indian treaties and federal Indian affairs statutes by states in *Worcester v. Georgia*,[196] where the court held that state law has no force in Indian country absent federal consent. Second, the Consti-tution established federal supremacy in Indian affairs.[197] Third, the Supreme Court decided *Dred Scott*. Fourth, Indian treaties estab-lished reserved rights to land, to resources, to water.[198] Fifth, Indian treaty rights are federal rights. Sixth, the Supreme Court in *United States v. Winans*,[199] an Indian treaty fishing case, and *Winters v. United States*,[200] an Indian water rights case, created the doctrine of federal reserved water rights. Seventh, the United States stopped a private dam from going up on the Rio Grande. Eighth, the Department of Justice retained a lawyer named William H. Veeder, and then later the Department of the Interior retained him. He wrote legal memoranda on Indian reserved rights and federal reserved water rights. Those memos, if CERF describes them correctly, pushed the United States to assert Indian rights to land, resources, and water in order to fulfill the federal–tribal trust responsibility. Ninth, Richard Nixon became president. Tenth, Barack Obama became president. Just about every rational person with knowledge would accept these facts.

Here are several conclusions CERF draws from these facts. No rational person should accept all of these conclusions, or perhaps any of them. First, according to CERF, "there is a Madisonian faction of federal attorneys that knows all of the facts and history but does not disclose this information to the federal courts when presenting arguments."[201] Here, CERF is alleging that any federal government attorney arguing in favor of Indian treaty rights is a "Madisonian faction." There really is no such thing as a "Madisonian faction." James Madison's definition of a "faction" in Federalist No. 10 was so broad as to include any group of people that argues against another group. Trade unions, Indians, and the Republican Party are all "Madisonian factions" in this way.

Second, "The *Dred Scott* ruling lives on because *Worcester* is still the law."[202] This one is baffling, and is likely an effort by CERF to distance itself from its well-known and well-documented racism by taking on the mantle of criticizing *Dred Scott*. The argument goes, I think, that the *Worcester* court prioritized federal law by applying the Supremacy Clause to the state of Georgia's anti-Indian laws. Federal law, as interpreted by the Supreme Court, also gave us the *Dred Scott* decision. This is an obvious logical fallacy. The Reconstruction Amendments eradicated *Dred Scott*. Federal law gives good and bad things, but it can no longer give us *Dred Scott*.

Third, "Tribal sovereignty is displacing federalism."[203] Well, tribal sovereignty is part of federalism. There's the federal government and there are the state governments. And then there are tribal governments. All three entities enjoy aspects of sovereignty. Article I, Section 8, Clause 3 of the US Constitution references both states and Indian tribes. The push and pull of sovereignty between these three types of governments is federalism. CERF ignores the very real state of cooperation between these three sovereigns, which is what federalism is all about.

Fourth, William H. Veeder "was a true believer in promoting and protecting Indian tribal rights."[204] This is not a problem. Federal officials can be true believers of all sorts of things.[205] Only Congress and federal agencies can act for the United States, not a lawyer working within the government. Besides, it's perfectly reasonable for a federal official to strongly recommend that the United States more aggressively fulfill its trust obligations to tribal interests.

Fifth, "By suppressing the information on William H. Veeder and what he wrote for the United States government, the Executive branch has created a true Madisonian faction of a small cadre of federal attorneys promoting his expanded trust concepts while not allowing the full constitutional ramifications of his ideas to be disclosed."[206] As noted before, no one knows for sure what a "Madisonian faction" is. A group of people sitting in a room bad-mouthing Indian tribes could be considered a faction. And no one is suppressing information about Mr. Veeder, who was a lawyer with relatively little authority when he was in government decades ago.

Finally, federal government attorneys, Richard Nixon, Barack Obama, the Ninth Circuit Court of Appeals, and presumably the hated Indian tribes, are conspiring to destroy America:

> Similarly the Ninth Circuit [in *United States v. Washington*] has now declared the Point Elliot Treaty to include sustenance rights just as William H. Veeder set out for the Nixon administration's Nixon Indian Policy. The Nixon Indian policy as the continuation of the federal reserved rights conspiracy now completely dominates our law. Only this Court can fix how this trust and reserved power have been combined to do this. There cannot be a separate equity authority that protects only Indians. To continue to so hold continues the Madisonian faction that is destroying our Constitution just as President Nixon hoped would happen.[207]

There is a lot here. Veeder perhaps did argue that the United States should advocate for Indian treaty rights. Perhaps he did argue that treaties created rights for Indian sustenance, or more accurately subsistence. So have virtually all federal government attorneys in the last century or more who have taken the trust responsibility seriously. Indian treaty negotiators did seek to establish permanent homelands, with rights to hunt, fish, gather, and farm – in other words, subsistence rights. The Puget Sound tribes are arguing in the *Washington* case that the treaties create a legal right to a homeland that allows Indian people the chance to fish for salmon, for subsistence. That likely means the state of Washington, and the United States as well, will have to fix the culverts it installed decades ago to ensure that salmon can spawn on streams affected by bad culverts. If these governments don't fix the culverts, Indian treaties will in fact be abrogated. It means salmon species will go extinct. It's difficult to see the destruction of America from this outcome.

The CERF brief ironically concludes with a condemnation of the US Supreme Court, effectively telling the justice that if the court does not proceed to dismantle Indian treaty rights and federal reserved rights altogether, the court is stupid and corrupt:

> Since the Civil War this Court has allowed federal attorneys to define the Constitution and spoon feed to the Justices the legal result they want in a decision. This Court has allowed lawyers representing the United States to define what is good or bad for the national government instead of this Court deciding what is best for preserving self-government and the rights of the people. This Court needs to be like an architectural board deliberately and carefully protecting the structure of the Constitution that literally keeps our civil rights and liberties intact. The utter failure of this Court has allowed a steady increase of federal authority across anything a federal attorney can claim as a federal interest.[208]

As a matter of persuasion, this is perhaps the single most idiotic strategy CERF could pursue. CERF alleges the Supreme Court as an institution isn't capable of assessing the validity of the federal government's arguments in litigation. Really, CERF is alleging that the court is in on the "conspiracy," too. CERF believes it's all the court's fault.

CERF knows this argument isn't going anywhere with the Supreme Court. There is no conspiracy of federal government attorneys. There is no "Madisonian faction." The Supreme Court is not stupid. Federal reserved water rights are controversial, yes, but they are no threat to the American people. Indian treaty rights are also controversial, but they are also no threat.

If anything, Indian treaty rights cases are about helping all Americans, all humans. Everyone in the Pacific Northwest, and anyone who likes to eat Pacific salmon, should support the Puget Sound tribes in their effort to preserve the habitat for salmon. In fact, the amicus briefs supporting the tribes might have sided with the CERF a half century ago in fighting treaty rights, but now they're siding with the tribes. This is also true in the Great Lakes, the northern plains, and elsewhere in Indian country, where tribes are fighting pipelines, invasive species, and air and water pollution. Earlier incarnations of CERF and CERA – and their current allies, like the Upstate Citizens for Equality – bled members after Indian tribes that were once targets of their animus started taking action to benefit all local people. Casinos might sound bad to some, but the money the tribes make spreads around to non-Indian employees, vendors, and governments. Tribal money funds environmental monitoring of air and water. Tribal money funds local schools, fire departments, law enforcement, public safety, cultural programs. The hate that led many non-Indians to show up at CERF/CERA meetings quickly dissipates when tribes become successful. Tribes hire former hate group members and their relatives, and generate economic activity that leads to jobs. It's much more difficult to blame Indians for your troubles when Indians and tribes are helping pay the rent. In the end, the only people left in these groups are the conspiracy people.

And if there is a conspiracy, it's not CERF's conspiracy. It's a conspiracy of industry and government to make it too easy to destroy the environment for profit. Industry money funds political action by federal and state governments. CERF cannot see this, or doesn't want to see it, so blinded are they by their hatred of Indians.

Conspiracy theorists live apart from the rest of society. They're constantly accusing others, constantly blaming others for their misfortunes, real and perceived. It's a vicious circle. They refuse to believe accepted facts. They see everyone as an enemy. In order to be conspiracy theorists, they absolutely have to live apart, like the deserted boy. CERF members will benefit from the tribal victory in *Washington v. United States*,[209] if they like to eat salmon, or drink clean water, or live apart from pipelines. But they fight Indians and tribes anyway, preferring to lose those resources rather than live with Indians in their midst. And like the deserted boy, Indian people reach out to their exiles, time and again. But CERF and their kind will always swat away the extended hand, preferring to burn the lodge down rather than live with Indians.

13

SQUABBLES IN LOCAL GOVERNMENT

There is the Anishinaabe story of the men who had no *ogema* (leader).[210] One of the men brought all of the Anishinaabe *ininiwaag* (men) together to smoke, to choose a leader. As the men smoked, the first man said, "All of the men and creatures of the earth have *ogimaag* (leaders), except us. We must choose a leader." The other men agreed, mulling over their smoke. The first man said, "I have brought this piece of fry bread. Once we choose a leader, the leader shall chew the fry bread." The others again agreed. They began to mull over who would be the *ogema*.

After a time, one man suggested another in the council. "Let him be *ogema*."

"No," said another. "He is a fool. What about him?" He pointed at a third man. "He is wise."

"Hardly," said the first man, thinking they would all have agreed by now that since he brought them together in council and he brought the sacred *semaa* (tobacco), he should be the *ogema*. But no one got to be leader by appointing themselves leader.

The Anishinaabe *ininiwaag* began to grumble. One *inini* eyed the fry bread. Others saw what he was doing.

The first man, the man who invited them all to council, was about to suggest himself as *ogema*, a tactic he knew would fail in a circle of flawed people like these, but his desire for power compelled him to try.

But then another man reached out and grabbed the fry bread. He took a bite. Another man leaned into the first man's face and bit down on the bread. This bread was not a particularly well-made piece of bread. It was hard and greasy, very chewy. The first man had made it himself. He could have asked his cousin, who was a much better cook, to make the bread, but he didn't want to answer any questions about why he needed bread. He didn't want anyone else in his family to know about the council.

Soon, three, then four *ininiwaag* were snarling and growling, teeth clamped on the chewy piece of poorly made fry bread. Spittle flecked out from the morass, along with bits and pieces of the bread. The men rolled around on the ground, clawing at each other, clawing at the ground to get a toehold, yelling and grunting like dogs.

The first man finally stood back and shook his head. "We are a council of dogs. None of us should lead. We are foolish and filled with envy." The rest of the men wrestled on the ground with their hands and feet and teeth until the bread was gone, and they were covered in scratches and sores.

Choosing leaders is not an easy task. In modern America, every day is election season. Congresspeople are up for election every two years. Same with many state legislative seats. Elections for municipal commissions, school boards, or tribal councils – even student body leadership positions – happen somewhere in America every month, every week. Most of these elections are far under the radar of national politics. Americans don't vote in national elections as much as they could. They tend to vote in local elections even less. The more local the election, the more likely we know the candidates. We might know their strengths, but we also know something about their weaknesses. I find myself in a voting booth often thinking something like, "Sure, Larry is a good guy, but he's not especially smart, and I know I would do a better job," or "Steph is a muckety-muck who just wants to be in people's business. Not sure she's my candidate." This is American democracy writ large.

San Juan County, Utah, politics is among the nastiest local politics in the United States. San Juan County is a sparsely populated area. About half of the residents are rural whites, and the other half are Navajo Nation citizens, Diné. Historically, San Juan County elected three county commissioners through a process known as at-large voting. At-large voting means the voters get three votes, and the three people with the largest tally win the election. Before the 1980s, that meant the three county commissioners were always non-Navajo whites. With a county leadership devoid of a Navajo voice, local political decisions always favored non-Navajos. Eventually, a Voting Rights Act suit brought by the United States in 1983 resulted in a settlement whereby San Juan County became a district voting jurisdiction, with the three seats assigned a specific territorial district. It ensured that at least one candidate favored by Navajo people would be elected, although Navajos will say that getting outvoted two-to-one on everything didn't change much.

So in the 2010s, the Navajo Nation brought another Voting Rights Act claim, this time arguing that packing all the Navajo citizens into one San Juan County district illegally discriminated against them on the basis of race.[211] The Navajo people prevailed. The federal district court judge ordered the drawing up of remedial districts that could allow two Navajos to win county commission and school board seats, and the federal appellate court affirmed.[212]

The political response from the San Juan County non-Navajos is a particularly virulent form of Indian-hating. In a blog post titled "San Juan County Citizens Facing Slavery and Racism,"[213] the anonymous writer, who many suspect is Monte Wells, a resident of San Juan County, places himself in perfect opposition to the "anti-liberty and freedom movement," or "ALFM." ALFM isn't a thing; the piece doesn't use this acronym again, nor does anyone else in the world. Wells, ostensibly speaking for non-Navajo voters in San Juan County, identifies with "freedom" and "liberty." And Wells assumes that those aligned with the Navajo Nation do not.

Of course, non-Navajo citizens of San Juan County are not about freedom or liberty at all. They couldn't be, or else they wouldn't compare themselves to Navajo people, who are descendants of people held in concentrations camps and forced to march to the death by

Americans in the nineteenth century. Called the Navajo Long Walk, it was really a series of more than fifty forced marches from what is now northern Arizona, western New Mexico, and, yes, San Juan County in southeastern Utah.[214] The United States, led by Kit Carson, destroyed the Navajo homelands, burning homes and crops and incarcerating Navajo people. The government then forced Navajos to walk unarmed and underfed to Bosque Redondo in what is now eastern New Mexico. There, the government incarcerated what was left of the Navajo Nation, about ten thousand people at first, in the 1860s. Conditions in the concentration camp were miserable. Starvation and disease were rampant, as well as murder and violent raids from other tribes. And slavery. The government eventually gave up the idea of concentrating the Navajos at Bosque Redondo, signed the Treaty of Fort Sumner in 1868,[215] and allowed the Navajo people to walk home, the return Long Walk. Americans look to the Revolutionary War as a founding national moment. The Navajos look to the Long Walk. If anyone knows about freedom and liberty, it is the descendants of these Navajo people.

Ironically, disgustingly, in the blog post's money quote, Wells literally alleges white citizens of San Juan County are about to be enslaved by the people of the Navajo Nation because of the redrawing of election districts:

> [The decision in *Navajo Nation v. San Juan County*] creates an outrageous situation of legalized plunder and a clear case of taxation without representation. This ruling by [Judge] Shelby is the Catullus [*sic*] that will strip all San Juan County citizens of their constitutional protection and rights. The result will be the creation of a welfare county of legalized plunder which will force us into involuntary servitude and slavery to the Navajo Nation. This is clearly a violation of the 13th Amendment.

There is a lot packed in this statement.

There is the dog whistle of "welfare,"[216] which for the white supremacist audience of the blog post means government services.

Wells's white supremacist audience believes the government services are funded by taxpayer dollars, with the taxpayers being exclusively white people. The white supremacist audience believes taxes are a form of legalized theft, where the government takes white people's money. The white supremacist audience assumes that the only beneficiaries of government programs are people of color, also known as welfare recipients. For the white supremacist, poor people of color, and possibly a few poor white people, are to blame for their poverty because they are inferior to hard-working whites. The kicker is that the white supremacist firmly believes there is a conspiracy by brown-skinned people to take over government, steal white people's money and property, and give it to other brown-skinned people. And probably the "abortionists" and the "gays," too.

It's worth noting what kind of government Monte Wells supports. He identifies and condemns or mocks gay rights, same-sex marriage, the Bears Ears National Monument, and the Recapture Canyon Protest trial (in which Wells was convicted of trespass and conspiracy). Wells does not support tribal government, which he says should have been disestablished by the 1924 Snyder Act[217] (presumably he means the 1921 Indian Citizenship Act;[218] the Snyder Act guarantees federal government services to American Indians). For Wells, terminating tribal governments would end the "complication of a nation within a nation." Besides, Wells notes, Utah finally allowed "non-Utah residents" – read: reservation Indians – to vote in 1957.[219]

It is apparently true that 60 percent of the land in the county is owned either by the United States or the Navajo Nation and its people. It is also apparently true that about half the population of San Juan County is Navajo. Before the most recent voting rights case, the San Juan County Commission was always majority non-Navajo. As described earlier, what this means is that about half the voters in San Juan County, white voters, always guaranteed that the commission and school board would be non-Navajo, hardly a sterling example of democracy. Much of the political power exercised by this minority of conservative whites, if Monte Wells is representative of that voting bloc, was exercised by attacking the federal government. It means, of course, that the power of the county is exercised by attacking Navajos. It was institutionalized, systemic Indian-hating.

The remedial districts are intended to create competitive political races in San Juan County. One can imagine a commission with two Navajos and one conservative white person. One can imagine a commission with one Navajo commissioner, one conservative white commissioner, and one moderate to liberal white commissioner. Who knows? The important part is that the power currently entrenched in San Juan County is dissolved in favor of a more diffuse power dynamic. Entrenched power is an enemy of the freedom and liberty Monte Wells insists is for him and his white supremacist audience, and for them alone.

In 2019, for the first time, Navajos outnumbered non-Navajos on the San Juan County Commission. Two Navajo men ran for San Juan County Commission, Kenneth Maryboy and Willie Greyeyes. Conservative politicians went after Willie Greyeyes, arguing that he was ineligible for office because he owned a trailer on the Arizona side of the border. The matter went to court, which found that Mr. Greyeyes had always lived on the Utah side. He owned the trailer from a time years earlier when he was sending his children to school in Arizona. It took a federal judge to order the commission's clerks to add Mr. Greyeyes's name to the ballot after they refused to do it.

The fry bread in the council of dogs story is the prize, of sorts, in any political campaign. The best governments are still imperfect. But in those governments, power is distributed around so that overarching power is not entrenched. The American Founders knew that. The entrenched power centers in San Juan County have forgotten that. They're wrestling over the fry bread, biting and clawing and barking for power they don't deserve. In traditional, and even modern Anishinaabe societies, the *ogema* who wins the fry bread gets to eat a chewy, greasy, hockey-puck hunk of bread. Leadership isn't really a prize and it shouldn't be a windfall. It's a burden. Leaders who seek the prize will always be distrusted by the people. Leaders who crave leadership for the power and prestige are simply the worst.

14

PRIVATIZING INDIAN LANDS

Great Lakes Anishinaabe used to tell stories about a horrific mystical creature known as the windigo.[220] The windigo was a tall, emaciated, desperately hungry spirit – a cannibal. The windigo roamed the deep woods, always looking to eat, never satisfied. Unending hunger was its curse. In the winter, the Anishinaabe would tell windigo stories from their lodges to remind each other about the sanctity and safety of their community, their kinship. The windigo, in these stories, started as an Anishinaabe person who went bad, who took too much from the community stores, who demanded more and more, who committed murder or other serious crimes, who could not be stopped, all in failed efforts to satiate their greed for more. Anishinaabe people needed each other to hunt and fish, to trade and barter, to plant and harvest the Three Sisters (corn, beans, and squash) and other crops. They needed each other for protection and to remember where their ancestors were buried. For Anishinaabe communities who depended on each other for companionship and sustenance, a selfish, greedy person was the worst of the worst.

Modern Anishinaabe people, like most American Indians, remember these ancient warnings about overconsumption. American Indian people form and operate tribal governments with an eye toward providing for the basic needs of everyone and everything in the community, especially elders and children. Indian people and their governments hold the land, the resources, and the sacred sites in the highest esteem and respect. Tribal governments make sustainability of Indian cultures, languages, economies, and resources the goal. We know what can happen when it goes bad, and windigos come.

Outsiders don't always understand the choices Indian people make in their governance philosophies. There are times when Indian nations depart from the generally accepted norms of American governance. At times, one supposes, the choices made by tribal governments and the Indian people who operate them can be downright terrifying to outsiders grounded in capitalism and profit, in American individualism and selfishness.

Since the 1980s and 1990s, as Indian tribes began to establish themselves, Indian-hating commentators have been advocating for the radical disestablishment of Indian tribes, of the federal–tribal trust relationship, and of Indian reservation land status.[221] These commentators make the claim that Indian country is poor because of a lack of "stable property rights and a stable rule of law."[222] The argument is basic. Indian lands are held in trust by the United States, or are in reservation status, and are largely inalienable absent federal consent. That federal control dampens Indian country economic development and growth. Indians are poor. Therefore, get rid of it all.

In recent years, commentators have been making a more specific case. This strategy involves opening up Indian country to unlimited and unregulated fossil fuel and mineral extraction, under the guise of helping Indian people. It's as if these commentators have never heard of the "resource curse," a term used by economists to describe how people living on natural resources suffer the great brunt of the impacts of extraction without really benefiting much from the value of the extracted resources. These commentators don't want to talk about the resource curse. They want the people living on these resources to think they're all going to get rich, like *The Beverly Hillbillies*. The reality behind these tales of reform is that they disguise a blueprint – not for Indians – but for non-Indian private interests to extract wealth from Indian lands. To paraphrase Spud in the movie *Trainspotting 2*, first the opportunity, then the betrayal.

This is a particularly insidious form of Indian-hating. Once again, non-Indians are trying to teach Indians how to kill the Indian in order to save the man.[223] At this writing, there is an Indian-hating businessman heavily dependent on fossil fuel and mineral interests for campaign cash, who is president of the United States and whose party is in control of the Senate, Indian-haters are becoming unusually aggressive. Under most other recent presidential administrations, the privatization radicals have been ever-present but quiet. Some tribes, whether influenced by the radicals or not, take the bait and open up their reservations to resources exploitation. We usually call these tribes "energy tribes." But with this administration, the privatization radicals (whose work is likely funded by fossil fuel and mineral extraction interests through private think tanks) might have the ear of national policy makers who could be interested in disestablishing the foundations of Indian law and policy in order to make a quick buck (or few billion quick bucks).

Let's examine the legal and political foundations of the problem, as explained by the privatization radicals. According to Regan and Anderson, who were publishing in 2014, "reservations contain almost 30% of the nation's coal reserves west of the Mississippi, 50% of potential uranium reserves, and 20% of known oil and gas reserves."[224] They suggest that billions upon billions of dollars of assets are buried in the ground on Indian lands. Importantly, they are nonspecific about which Indian reservations hold these supposed assets. The most active energy tribes include the Navajo Nation, Crow Nation, Hopi Tribe, Southern Ute, and Mandan, Hidatsa, Arikara Nation, and a few others. These tribes are already deep in the business of extracting fossil fuels and minerals. Most of them face enormous internal political pressures from their own citizens to stop because they're destroying their homelands, their sacred sites, their futures. Other than perhaps the Southern Ute, all of these tribes face enormous poverty despite exploiting their natural resources for profit. By the way, the non-Indian energy companies are doing just fine. They don't live on the lands that have been torn apart and polluted for ten thousand years by resource extraction.

Privatization radicals demand that other tribes join the active energy tribes in shredding and polluting their reservations. For these commentators, especially people like Naomi Schaefer Riley,[225] tribes that don't open up their reservations to non-Indian exploitation are either stupid or corrupt. Or the federal government is holding them back.

For privatization radicals, the federal government is evil. Not just in Indian affairs, but everywhere. Some antigovernment people sound like conspiracy theorists when they complain about the government,[226] kind of like Agent Mulder in *The X-Files*. But in Indian law, the federal government's presence really is considerable. And that's a good thing. Here's the story.

One of the primary goals of the United States at its founding was to liberate Indian people from their land and resources. A good deal of Indian-hating derives from the conflicts that inevitably arose as non-Indians sought to take, and took, Indian-owned resources. Indian land holdings shrank dramatically every year until well into the late-twentieth century. First came the land cession treaties that allowed western territories to become states. Then came the reservations, larger at first, then whittled down again and again, sometimes to nothing, by federal actions carving them up. Then came allotment, in which the federal government carved up what was left of the reservations, intentionally breaking up the tribal land mass.[227] Then came termination in the 1940s and 1950s, where the Department of the Interior and Congress, helped along by Congress, confiscated Indian lands and resources directly and terminated the trust relationship between the United States and more than two hundred Indian tribes (Congress did eventually restore most, but not all, of these terminated tribes).

Remedies for these losses have been a sorry collection of laws and policies that have helped stop the bleeding of Indian lands and resources but have allowed for relatively little to be restored to tribes. The key laws are the Non-Intercourse Act and the Indian Reorganization Act. The Non-Intercourse Act,[228] which dates back to 1790, prohibits the alienation of Indian reservation lands without consent of Congress. Section 5 of the Indian Reorganization Act,[229] authorizes the secretary of the interior to acquire land in trust for Indian tribes and individual Indians. That trust land also cannot be alienated without federal approval. It's fair to say that in the modern era, reservation and trust lands cannot be alienated without tribal approval, either.

What this means is that much of Indian country has a restriction on alienation. In federal Indian law terms, reservation and trust lands are under federal superintendency. Other federal laws restrict or regulate contracts with Indian tribes[230] and leases with Indian tribes,[231] for example. There is a lot of bureaucracy. An Indian person usually cannot own reservation lands or trust lands controlled by an Indian tribe, and the ability to collateralize those lands is extremely difficult. What it also means is that Indian tribes have control over a lot of land in which they can provide basic human services to Indian people and allow for the protection and development of their tribal cultures.

Privatization radicals condemn that entire system as antithetical to capitalism. They already condemn government regulations anyway, and the kind of government regulation they see in Indian country must make them crazy. Privatization radicals see only one solution – gut the system, replace it with uncontrolled capitalism and unregulated property rights. Naomi Schaefer Riley referred to property rights as "magical."[232] In Indian country, to believe that uncontrolled capitalism and unregulated property rights will do much to solve poverty isn't magic, it's magical thinking.

Consider the Oglala Sioux Tribe, located on the Pine Ridge Reservation in present-day South Dakota, perhaps the reservation most devastated by poverty in the United States. That tribe has no exploitable natural resources, at least not on the scale of any of the energy tribes. There are a bunch of Indians and non-Indians who own land on the reservation who would love privatization. But they probably wouldn't get rich, and the rest of the Pine Ridge reservation residents would get nothing at all. The tribe and its people are the tribe closest to the Black Hills, though, and they desperately wants the Black Hills restored to tribal control. No one knows for sure, but one can't help but think the restoration of the Black Hills to tribal control could turn the tide in favor of Indian people.

Privatization radicals don't care about Pine Ridge at all. They like to use the poverty statistics generated there to complain about federal and tribal governments, but privatization isn't going to help the Oglala Sioux people much at all. What privatization will do, almost certainly, is terminate the tribal government, or at least gut it completely. Those privatization radicals won't be there to theorize about how Pine

Ridge people can pick up the pieces. If anything, they'll congratulate themselves on destroying a government. Oh, and they will preach to the victims of privatization that their own moral failings are the reason they're suffering.

Many of the poorest Indian people are Alaska Natives. Many of the Alaska Native villages once had control over their natural resources, but they lost control over those resources when Congress created Alaska Native Corporations in 1971's Alaska Native Claims Settlement Act.[233] The corporations and their shareholders control – and handsomely profit from – those lands and resources, leaving far too many Indian people poor. Where are the privatization radicals' solutions for Alaska? We hear only crickets from them about Alaska. There are no solutions because privatization radicals are satisfied with Alaska. They are satisfied with poverty for Alaska Natives, especially since they can count Alaska Native poverty in the statistics they use to criticize federal and tribal governments. And they absolutely do.[234]

Privatization radicals are modern-day windigos. They lurk in the shadows, hovering around Indian people, always hungry, famished. They eat, they consume, they murder (they are cannibals, after all), but it is never enough. Even Nanaboozhoo was terrified of windigos.

There are many stories of great courage in which Anishinaabe people fought windigos. The stories I find most inspiring are those where a young Anishinaabe *kwe* (woman) defeated a windigo.[235] There's something magical about young Indian women that makes them perfect for fighting supernatural monsters. Maybe it's because young women are new to their womanhood and the power that accompanies it. Maybe it's because Indian women are more protective of home, community, and family. Maybe it's because Indian women are smarter.

The future for many Indian communities is in youth, and in women. I've been to a fair number of meetings where Indian leaders of energy tribes are expounding on their economies and promoting their resource exploitation efforts. A half century ago and earlier, they used to call tribal leaders of large, landed reservations – almost all of them men – the "big bellies." Today, the overwhelming majority of energy tribe leaders, attorneys, and specialists speaking out in favor of more exploitation of Indian lands are men.

Conversely, when I attend meetings where Indian people are talking about climate change, sustainable economies, and children and families, the overwhelming majority of speakers and leaders are Indian women. I much prefer those meetings.

I'm siding with the windigo fighters.

15

EVERY TWO YEARS AT A SITE SOME DISTANCE AWAY: INDIAN-HATERS ON INDIAN RELIGIONS

Northern Michigan Anishinaabe people know the story about how the Sleeping Bear dunes were formed.[236] In this story, a mother *mukwa* (bear) and her two cubs were living in Wisconsin. There was a terrible drought going on there. Everything was dead or dying. The mother bear and the two cubs were starving. In another telling, a massive forest fire had engulfed their home in Wisconsin. Either way, desperate to escape, the mother bear formed a plan for the small family to swim across Lake Michigan to reach Michigan territory where there might be food and shelter. So they began swimming. They swam and swam. Already weak from their starvation, it was slow going. The mother bear was just getting along, but the cubs were struggling. They swam on, and eventually they could see the Michigan shoreline. But one cub stopped swimming. No matter how much the mother bear tried to help, the bear cub could not go on. And the cub drowned. The second bear cub also began to struggle. And shortly after the first cub drowned, the second cub drowned. The heartbroken mother bear kept on, finally reaching the shore. Exhausted and devastated, the mother bear fell asleep on the shore. She is still there today. Her cubs formed North and South Manitou Islands. The mother bear became the Sleeping Bear dunes.

If it weren't already obvious, these locations are deeply sacred to the Anishinaabe people. The *mukwa* is a deeply spiritual animal, with a close connection to the Anishinaabe. It is one of the seven core clans of the

Anishinaabe people. The *mukwa dodem* (clan) is the clan charged with policing the community. *Mukwa* clan members are well respected by the Anishinaabe people.

Perhaps tied to the responsibilities of the bear clan, or perhaps not, another story involves the Sleeping Bear dunes.[237] In this story, an Anishinaabe *inini* (man) was traveling by *jiimaan* (canoe) on Lake Michigan along the Beaver Island, Fox Islands, and Manitou Islands archipelago. Back then, the Anishinaabe used landmarks on the shoreline to navigate. Waganakising and its crooked tree was one such landmark. The Sleeping Bear dunes were another. The Anishinaabe *inini* stopped to camp at the big dune facing the lake. For one to climb the big dune is to assure that one will live a long life. The top of the dune is hundreds of feet above the beach, and the angle is ridiculously steep. To walk up is to court madness. Almost all progress is lost with every step, as the sand gives way. Only the strongest and most patient people reach the top. In this story, the Anishinaabe *inini* showed he was strong and patient. He passed by other Anishinaabe who attempted the climb, but made it only partway up. When our Anishinaabe *inini* reached the top, the spirits assured him he would live a long life, a good life.

Sacred sites in Indian country all have their own story. Indian stories attached to a location often detail critical information important to the lifeways of Indian people. I think the story about the formation of Sleeping Bear dunes is one of those stories. The story reminds Anishinaabe about the bond between parents and children, and how terrible it can be for that bond to be broken. Michigan Anishinaabe families broken apart by the removals of Indian children from their families, removals that date back to the early nineteenth century and continue today, might look at Sleeping Bear dunes differently from non-Indian visitors.

I think it is also important that the story of the dunes is about the *mukwa dodem* (bear clan), the first and last line of defense for Anishinaabe communities. *Mukwa dodem* people are strong and fierce.

Climbing Sleeping Bear dunes is a reasonable test for them. But *mukwa dodem* people are not mere soldiers. They are protectors. They must counsel their strength with wisdom, with humility and love. Climbing Sleeping Bear dunes is also a test of patience, another good test for *mukwa dodem* people.

Mukwa dodem people make for good lawyers as well. *Waabizheshi dodem* (marten clan) and *meshike dodem* (turtle clan) also make for good lawyers. *Waabizheshi dodem* people are in the same grouping as *mukwa dodem*, the martial clans. *Waabizheshi dodem* people are *ogitchida*, warriors. *Meshike dodem* people are speakers – good for lawyering, too. Anishinaabe from other clans are also good for lawyering, but perhaps these clans have the most natural fit. Still, *mukwa dodem* and *waabizheshi dodem* people must learn to temper their strength in order to be great lawyers. Stories like the ones involving Sleeping Bear dunes can teach modern Anishinaabeg a lot.

As an Anishinaabe lawyer, I have worked for other Indian tribes. One of those tribes was the Hoopa Valley Tribe. The Hoopa Valley Tribe Reservation, known locally as the Hoopa Square, is in a mountainous, timber-rich area three hundred miles or so north of San Francisco. That tribe's citizens have a much different culture from the Anishinaabe culture I am used to, but there are still many commonalities, especially compared to American culture. I learned about the importance of the black bear to the Hoopa, or Hupa, people. The Hoopa Square is inundated with black bears. While I worked there, black bears had begun to ruin portions of the Hupa timber assets, and the tribe was in a debate about how to deal with them. The most obvious response, advocated by non-Hupa tribal employees, was to pare down the black bear population through hunting and trapping. Traditional Hupas told me they were opposed to that plan. More so than with the Anishinaabe, who consider bears to be a relative, Hupas think of bears as brothers, almost human. Some told me they had seen what a bear looks like when it is killed and skinned – it looks just like a human, albeit a human with claws and a snout. This kind of community debate became political, and there were powerful voices on all sides.

The Hoopa Valley Tribe, like most other tribes, engages in spirited democratic debate. Words are said, things are done, injuries are inflicted on some community members. The tribe is also closely related to nearby tribes, including the Yurok Tribe, the Karuk Tribe, the Klamath Tribe, and the Tolowa Nation. There is a lot of intertribal conflict, including intergenerational conflict over the Hoopa Square. A lot of bad will can build up over time at Hoopa, both internally and externally.

Hupa culture deals with the buildup of bad will, conflict, and angry voices by holding a world-cleansing ceremony called the White Deerskin Dance. They hold this weeks' long ceremony every two years. Each of the eight or so Hupa family groups hosts a portion of the ceremony at different locations. The ceremony moves from location to location until concluding near an area called Bald Hill. The specific locations are secret, although they tend to be located within the same area, or what are called "fields" at Hoopa. They're in heavily forested, isolated areas. Outsiders might be invited to participate, but they must be escorted, and are expected to not reveal the location of the part of the ceremony they visit.

In the 1990s, the tribal council began a process to create laws and regulations that would protect those locations, those sacred sites. All but about three percent of the Hoopa Square was owned by the tribe, and most of the non-Hupa-owned land was located near the town of Hoopa on the Trinity River, away from the sacred locations. Still, the tribe was worried that either the state of California or the US Department of the Interior would either inadvertently or intentionally authorize the logging of timber on or near the various secret locations of the White Deerskin Dance. Recall those locations are intentionally secret, so even the state and federal governments don't know where they are located. The tribe was also trying to protect those locations from its own citizens, and itself. The biggest logging company on the reservation is, after all, owned by the tribe. The tribe proposed a series of laws and regulations creating buffer zones that would protect the sacred locations. The tribe asked for comments from the state and federal agencies and looked for ways to cooperate with all affected governments and property owners. They held hearings to describe their plans and to hear comments from the public. In 1995, the state and federal government agencies agreed to cooperate. And so the tribe enacted the buffer zone legislation.

A non-Indian person named Roberta Bugenig purchased about forty acres of forested land within the Hoopa Square, partially located within one of the buffer zones. She refused at first to acknowledge the reality that she was located within an Indian reservation. She asked for permission from the state of California to log a few small acres of her parcel, and state officials, either ignorant of or forgetting about the Hoopa buffer zones, initially approved her application. They quickly, though not quickly enough, backtracked and told her to seek tribal approval. Bugenig knew she wouldn't receive approval from the tribe, but she did send in an application to the tribe for a license, along with a check, to drive logging trucks on tribal highways. The tribe sent back the check and the application. Bugenig commenced logging anyway, ultimately clear-cutting the entire forty-acre parcel. That timber probably was worth a tidy sum.

The tribe sued Bugenig in tribal court, seeking to enforce its buffer zone regulations. They presented extensive testimony from Hupa traditional people and historical experts, detailing the importance of the White Deerskin Dance to the Hupa people. The tribe created a monumental factual record of this material in the tribal court. The trial court opinion, and later the tribal appellate court opinion, was replete with the justification for the buffer zones. The tribal judiciary enjoined Bugenig's logging activities.[238] Sadly, while the litigation was ongoing, Bugenig was clear-cutting her entire parcel in violation of tribal laws.

After the tribal court issued its final decision, Bugenig challenged the jurisdiction of the tribal court over her and her land in federal court.[239] The federal district court rejected her claim, holding that the tribe had the power to regulate logging by both Indians and non-Indians on the Hoopa Square. But on appeal to the Ninth Circuit Court of Appeals, the tribe initially lost.

A lot of people think the Ninth Circuit is the most liberal circuit in the federal judiciary. It is true that there are a fair number of actual liberal judges on that court, but the entire circuit includes a roster of dozens of judges that run the ideological gamut. Some of the most conservative judges in the federal judiciary are also on the Ninth Circuit. For each appeal, the Ninth Circuit randomly assigns a panel of three judges to hear it. In any given appeal, that panel of three might be incredibly conservative. Worse for tribal interests, some of the more liberal judges are fairly skeptical of tribal powers. Other judges who might be liberal or moderate are completely uninterested in cases involving tribal interests. When Roberta Bugenig appealed to the Ninth Circuit, the three judges assigned to her appeal formed a perfect storm of Indian-hating more than the sum of its parts, Diarmuid O'Scannlain, Thomas Reavely, and Ronald Gould.[240] O'Scannlain was a conservative star, a Reagan appointee, with a long history of writing opinions deeply critical of federal Indian law and tribal interests. Gould was a Clinton appointee, at that time a brand-new judge, and is still considered an unusually liberal judge. But for some reason, Judge Gould has a history of skepticism regarding tribal interests. Judge Reavely, a Texan, was a Carter appointee to the Fifth Circuit with no experience in Indian affairs – not a likely candidate to stand up for the Hoopa Valley Tribe in the face of concerted hostility to tribal interests even if he had wanted to do so.

Judge O'Scannlain wrote the panel opinion in *Bugenig v. Hoopa Valley Tribe*. The panel completely ignored the tribal court record describing in great detail the importance of the White Deerskin Dance, a cultural and religious ceremony critically important to the continued health of the tribe's community. Instead, the panel fundamentally insulted the tribe's culture with the following callous remark: "Simply stated, any arguable impact that cutting second-growth timber might have upon the holding of a tribal dance once every two years, at a site some distance away, 'has no potential to affect the health and welfare of a tribe in any way approaching the threat [required to justify tribal jurisdiction over non-Indians.]'"[241] Instead of acknowledging the critical importance to the Hupa people of the world-cleansing event that is the White Deerskin Dance, the court mocked the ceremony as a mere "dance" that happens once every two years.

The panel decision in Bugenig was problematic enough for a majority of the Ninth Circuit active judges that the circuit agreed to hear the appeal in a larger panel of eleven judges (lawyers call that an "en banc" panel). The en banc panel reversed the original panel opinion but on different grounds. Even that court didn't do much to recognize the legal importance of the White Deerskin Dance to the Hupa people. But at least the principle that the Hoopa Valley Tribe can regulate lands within the buffer zone, regardless of the race of the owner, was confirmed.

Many American Indian religions and cultures are rooted in a place. Anishinaabe law is rooted in a place, too. Given that so much Indian culture is tied to a location, those places take up enormous space in the imaginations and passions of Indian people. In some Indian religions, like the White Deerskin Dance, you have to be at that location in order to receive the spiritual and emotional benefit from the ceremony. The Hupa people, wherever they might be at a given time, must be a little more secure after the *Bugenig* ruling that their sacred sites are protected by their own tribal government, on their very own reservation. Indian people have always celebrated and prioritized the places where they hold their ceremonies and where they have buried their ancestors. Many, maybe most, tribal communities don't have that security. Perhaps the federal government removed them from their traditional homelands, their ceremonial grounds, their burying grounds. Perhaps the federal government took those places and kept them as federal public lands, claiming ownership over sacred sites and burial grounds on behalf of all Americans, a truly twisted outcome. Or perhaps the government took those lands and gave them away, sold them to political constituents. The stories of the loss of Indian sacred sites are voluminous.

For a long time, the big dune at Sleeping Bear held steady at 234 feet. The dune has steadily and dramatically eroded away. By 1980, it stood at about 100 feet. The dune is now part of the Sleeping Bear Dunes National Lakeshore, ostensibly protected by federal law and the park rangers who enforce that law. But each summer day, hundreds of people climb up and down the dune, wearing it away even more. Fewer and fewer Anishinaabe people from northwest lower Michigan learn the origin story of the sleeping bear, and fewer still know of the relationship between the big dune and Anishinaabe leadership and clan structures.

This is a sad story, much like the loss suffered by the mother *mukwa*. Maybe now the story is more about loss than anything else.

16

THE AMERICAN CONSTITUTIONALISTS VERSUS THE HAUDENOSAUNEE CONFEDERACY INFLUENCE THEORY

The Anishinaabeg tell a story about a giant, a wizard, a magician, or a powerful man named Mashos.[242] He is a selfish, brutal man, who jealously guards his daughters. One day, a young Anishinaabe man with great skill and wisdom appears at the village. Mashos's daughter and the young man fall in love. The rest of Mashos's family, his wife, his other children, and even the other people in the village, approve of the coupling. The young man is a skilled hunter, a caring and loving suitor, and a good citizen. He would make the village richer and more secure. Mashos reluctantly agrees to the marriage, but secretly plots the death of his son-in-law. Mashos is a gatekeeper, blinded by his obsession with maintaining power, control, and prestige, even if it harms his daughter, his family, his community. Mashos is a monster.

First as a lawyer, and then an academic, I have come to learn there are many gatekeepers. Gatekeepers are not inherently monstrous or wrong. They perform important functions, but there is an inherent risk of abuse in any gatekeeping function. As a lawyer, I learned judges are gatekeepers (interestingly enough, most of my law practice now is as a tribal judge). I learned in-house counsel for Indian tribes are gatekeepers of legal expertise for that tribe. As an academic, I learned that senior academics in one's field are incredibly powerful gatekeepers. Luckily for me, the scholars in my field of American Indian law who advised me were generous, humble, and wise. They took a lot of time to read my draft papers, to walk me through the tenure process, and even to talk me up to others. When reading my draft papers, my mentors and advisors looked to see if my claims were novel and whether they were important or useful. They looked to see whether I used proper evidence to back up my claims. They looked to see if my writing was adequate enough to communicate my ideas to others. As I transition into a senior scholar, I shall do my best to perform the same service to junior scholars, to do so in line with Mino-Bimaadiziwin.

Not all academic gatekeepers are as generous and humble. Instead, in most other fields, I believe, the primary code words are *rigor* and *objectivity*. There's nothing inherently wrong with rigor and objectivity. First as a political commentator, and later as an academic, Vine Deloria, Jr. was known for his tough love with other Native scholars, so much so that a recent book about his intellectual thought describes it as "punishing."[243] My own mentors would say they looked at my work for evidence of rigor and objectivity. But in the history of academic gatekeeping, rigor and objectivity have too often been applied as a hammer to destroy junior scholars with original ideas and methods. Or they are tools to reach across ideologies as a hammer to destroy scholars with whom one passionately disagrees.

As might be obvious by now, academic gatekeepers can facilitate Indian-hating. Until recent decades, almost all academics in the United States were religious white men. These men learned their history of the West from the scholarship of people like Samuel Eliot Morison, who taught them that Indians were violent heathens whom American superiority conquered, subhumans who could never be assimilated. They learned their law from people like Christopher Columbus Langdell, who taught them that Indians were savages without law. They learned their politics from people like Andrew Jackson, who taught them that American white men knew best how to deal with Indians, who could never understand reason and would only listen to the man with the sword or the rifle. They learned their arts from people like James Fenimore Cooper, who taught them that Indians were romantic and noble, but a vanishing race probably better off dead. Americans in power have subsumed these ideas for centuries, from the time they learn about the first Thanksgiving to the time they see their first John Wayne cowboy movie to the time they see Indians on the news singing in tongues while protesting a core American activity like building pipelines. Anyone who dared challenge these broad principles at Harvard or in Washington, D.C., or in Hollywood presumptively was completely wrong, possibly insane, likely incompetent, and downright dangerous.

Yet, because of people like Vine Deloria, Jr., Don Fixico, Elizabeth Cook-Lyn, Duane Champagne, Louise Erdrich, and Rennard Strickland, there is a place in many scholarly fields for Indian scholars to incubate. As a law scholar, I owe enormous debts to Vine, whom I never met, and Rennard, whom I have met only once or twice, for paving my way and carving safe places for me to research, write, think, publish, and speak. Currently, there are a couple dozen American Indian people who are law professors, an absolutely tiny number of people. But we make a lot of noise.

Academia has come a long way, but the presumptions against Indian people remain. Indian scholars see it all over the place. Legal scholars see it when the chief justice of the United States angrily slaps down the attorney for an Indian tribe who refers to tribal lands as a homeland, because his homeland is America, not Indian country. Political scholars see it when the president of the United States refers to a political opponent as "Pocahontas." Creative arts scholars see it when almost all representations of Indian people in movies and television are of casino operators, rather than a wide variety of people who are professionals. In our safer places, Native scholars don't have to answer questions or counter remarks that are casually racist or ignorant. In the larger academic world, which is a highly politicized world, Native scholars must respond almost constantly to casual Indian-hating. There are many scholarly and political questions involving Indian people that are passionately contested; for example, the Bering Strait bridge theory, the Ancient One (also known as Kennewick Man), tribal powers over nonmembers, cultural repatriation of ancestors and sacred objects, and cultural appropriation, just to name a few. These are fairly important questions, with real-world implications.

But weirdly enough, the scholarly question that has generated intensely passionate, even pathological arguments, involves no real-world implications at all, at least in my view. The question that makes some intellectuals so incredibly angry is whether the Haudenosaunee Confederation influenced the drafting of the American Constitution.

The classic story of the framing of the US Constitution is the mythology of the formation of a more perfect union by enlightened and brilliant thinkers.[244] The Founders, especially James Madison, the father of the Constitution, supposedly weighed the interests of each of the thirteen states against the need for a national government. There was a great compromise, there were checks and balances, and there was separation of powers. Most Americans don't know much about, and usually don't want to talk about, how the Constitution addressed slavery and Indian tribes. What many Americans do know is that the Framers enabled the continuation of slavery, leaving that horrifying institution and culture for future generations to deal with. Hardly any Americans know how the Constitution dealt with Indians and tribes. In high school civics class, to the extent American public school students are paying attention, they will learn about federalism, the structure of government that in many ways defines American government, a split of powers between the states and the federal government.

In the 1970s, we know anecdotally, a legal anthropology scholar named Laura Nader popularized the idea that the one of the most influential Framers of the American Constitution, Benjamin Franklin, took the idea of federalism from the Haudenosaunee Confederacy. Centuries ago, the Haudenosaunee nations – the Mohawk, Onondaga, Oneida, Seneca, Cayuga, and (later) Tuscarora Nations – warred amongst each other constantly until they formed a confederacy with a written constitution, the Great Law of Peace, long before the influence of Christopher Columbus and those who followed reached the world of the Haudenosaunee people. One key principle in the Great Law of Peace was that no nation would fight against another, and that if there was to be war against another nation, all of the Haundenosaunee nations must agree unanimously. Each of the individual nations had plenary control over their internal matters, but when it came to outside matters, the nations met together in a longhouse to address them collectively. This was a powerful and efficient mechanism that withstood the test of centuries, at least until the American Revolution, when the Haudenosaunee Confederacy did split.

This is not going to be the place to detail the arguments for and against the Haudenosaunee influence theory. What interests me is the impact of the influence theory on mainstream historians and legal scholars. Gordon Wood, an American historian of the Revolution period so influential that Matt Damon and Ben Affleck name checked him in the *Good Will Hunting* screenplay, attacked a junior legal historian, a woman, for not sufficiently rejecting the Haudenosaunee influence theory:

> Alison LaCroix, Assistant Professor of Law at The University of Chicago Law School . . . does grant some credibility to this idea that the Iroquois Confederacy contributed to America's conception of union before concluding that "on balance . . . the case for causation has not been made. . . ." This seems to me to be much too generous: this strange case for causation ought to have been dismissed out of hand. LaCroix thinks of herself as a historian, and no historian would conceive of causation or influence in this simple-minded manner. The Iroquois and other Indians certainly contributed a great deal to early American culture, but ideas about federalism were not among their contributions.[245]

He began his attack on Alison LaCroix by invoking another woman, Laura Nader, whom he similarly did not respect as a scholar, referring to her as "an angry woman" who pointed him to documents detailing the influence theory.[246] Wood likely thought of himself as the preeminent modern-day scholar of the Revolution and the framing, the most powerful gatekeeper of the history of the American founding. Needless to say, his nasty attack on a junior scholar was a bit much, an elder man calling into question with a mocking tone the credibility of a younger woman. His attack on two women, one who actively argued in favor of the theory, and another who merely mentioned it, but not on the dozens of other scholars, generally men, who have advanced the theory, perhaps highlights the misogynist aspects of American scholarly gatekeeping, but that is for another time.

For Wood, even harboring the possibility that there was something behind the Haudenosaunee influence theory was tantamount to academic malpractice at worst, and incompetence at best. Nothing in LaCroix's work depended on the influence theory,[247] so Wood's emphasis on that question was irrelevant. But it speaks a lot about Indian-hating. Wood didn't bother to debunk the influence theory, either, concluding that it "ought to [be] dismissed out of hand." In short, for Wood, the Haundenosaunee influence theory was so out-of-bounds as to not be deserving of a response.

And yet Wood acknowledged that the Haudenosaunee nations and people "contributed a great deal to early American culture." Perhaps Wood was thinking about Cooper's *Last of the Mohicans*, a monumental contribution to American culture, although one can and should question whether Cooper's representation of the Haudenosaunee people is relevant in the twenty-first century. But it is odd for Wood to demand ideological and methodological purity from Alison LaCroix while in the same paragraph casually admitting the Haudenosaunee people had oversized influence on the early American Republic. Constitution and culture. That's a thing. A constitution without cultural backing is a dead letter. A constitution without a mythology, as well, is a dead letter. There's a story there, but Gordon Wood is too busy trying to smash down women who do not toe his ideological line.

Wood isn't the only academic departing from the usual academic rigor in his effort to attack the Haudenosaunee influence theory. Consider Erik M. Jensen, a law professor who was so incensed by a pair of footnotes in a student-authored law review article that he dedicated an entire article of his own to abusing the authors, a paper that quickly devolved into a series of statements mocking the Haudenosaunee people.[248] Like Wood, Jensen concludes the influence theory is wrong, "wishful thinking, nothing more," and "it should disappear from scholarly discourse."[249] And because wishing no scholar would mention the influence theory ever again apparently isn't enough, Jensen adds that the theory is "dumb," "shouldn't be propped up by citations in the *Harvard Law Review*," "grounded in quicksand," "close to a world record for implausibility," and "indefensible."[250] To be fair, the bit about the quicksand was referring to the thesis of the student article, which Jensen argues would be subject to the metaphorical horror of sinking slowly into the kind of wet, slimy pond scum that plagued every adventuring archaeologist this side of Indiana Jones if it relied on the influence thesis.

But like Alison LaCroix, the student authors aren't citing the Haudenosaunee influence thesis as the foundation for their argument, just a small part of it. Jensen isn't satisfied that they "didn't explicitly say they were endorsing the influence thesis;" he wants a full-throated condemnation of the thesis, or at least he wants it "summarily rejected."[251] Oddly, it takes several pages for Jensen to satisfactorily (in his mind apparently) destroy the influence thesis, which is by definition somewhat more than summarily. Decades ago, Jensen had written a more fully developed article that justified summary rejection of the influence thesis, labeling the thesis with the damning adjective "imaginary."[252]

Here is the Haudenosaunee influence thesis that Jensen wants to eliminate from scholarly discourse altogether. In 1750 or 1751, Benjamin Franklin wrote a letter in which he noted that the Haudenosaunee confederacy had "subsisted ages, and appears indissoluble," and could be a model for a union of the colonies.

Jensen says there is no evidence whatsoever in the history of the world that American colonists and Indians would ever have engaged in discussions of political theory. He argues that because there was so much hostility between the two groups that as soon as a white man and an Indian saw each other, they'd likely begin fighting to the death. Indians and colonists were not "friendly," there were "tensions," and Indian–colonial relations were "hostile." The American Framers really hated Indians and therefore never would have let Indian philosophy infect American political theory. Consider the Declaration of Independence, these scholars argue, which famously references the British Crown's failure to protect Americans from "merciless Indian savages." Or Federalist No. 24, where Alexander Hamilton condemned the "savage tribes." The scholars argue that there is no way the Framers would have taken the political theory of "merciless Indian savages" or "savage tribes" seriously when crafting an organic document for a civilized republic. Jensen underscores this portion of the argument in a parenthetical "(Would a rational new nation take its governing principles from merciless savages or savage tribes?)"[253] In short, no "rational" colonist or Framer would take their ideas seriously. Jensen adds that Benjamin Franklin thought Indians were complete morons, and so there's no way in Jensen's mind a rational thinker like Benjamin Franklin would have taken their government as a model for much of anything. Jensen concludes, "Yes, Franklin urged consolidation of the colonies, but his urging was in the nature of 'if even the ignorant Iroquois can do it, of course we can.'"[254]

This is the opening gambit in the anti-influence thesis crowd, that the Framers and Indians hated each other, so there really couldn't have been any kind of intellectual sharing between the two groups. But that's not enough. There's a second part of the anti-influence-thesis thesis, "proven" with a liberal sprinkling of statements that reek with Indian-hating. Jensen, for example, suggests that the colonists probably didn't know much about the Haudenosaunee law anyway because it was written as wampum (memory beads), and "translations of wampum weren't available to the American founders."[255] Jensen then mocks Barbara Mann, a scholar who reported that the earliest date of the Great Law of Peace was August of 1142, for relying on Haudenosaunee oral tradition. Jensen sarcastically ridicules the "precision" of that date:

> How do we know that August 1142 – what a nice sense of precision! – was "perhaps" a key date? According to the *Encyclopedia*, it's because of oral tradition – you know, passing stories from one generation to the next, with embellishment inevitably occurring along the way [think John Smith and Pocahontas, Washington and the cherry tree, Eliot Ness and the Untouchables] – and tying certain events to solar eclipses, particularly one that occurred on August 31, 1142 (more precision!): "The Keepers speak of a Black Sun (total eclipse) that occurred immediately before the league was founded."[256]

Jensen's not finished, because he tosses in doubts that Indian tribes had anything approaching governments that "rational" American colonists would have appreciated. He finds "perversely interesting" the law students' claim that there was any Indian political theory at all.[257]

Savages. Merciless. Ignorant. Bad timekeepers. In Jensen's words, "What were the *Harvard Law Review* people thinking in letting this stuff appear in their pages?"[258]

The Haudenosaunee influence thesis, whether or not it had any historical merit, serves a critically important purpose. First, the passion it inspires brings out the academic gatekeepers. Laura Nader's attack on Gordon Wood for not acknowledging the Haudenosaunee influence led to Wood's counterattack on Nader and his attack on Alison LaCroix. The Harvard law students' casual embrace of the influence theory brought out an overwrought response from Erik Jensen fit more for the comments section of the Volokh Conspiracy, a conservative law blog known for vituperative debate, than the pages of the *British Journal of American Legal Studies*. That the mere possibility of Indian influence on the godlike Framers of the American Constitution generates such heated academic exchange really is remarkable. Indian-hating is a real thing.

Second, the substance of the arguments against the Haudenosaunee influence theory highlight more specifically how Indian-hating lives on in the twenty-first century. Stereotyping Indian people as uncivilized and stupid, pagan and violent, is a long-standing American pastime. Anti-influence scholars are devastatingly quick to attribute ethnocentric and outright racist beliefs to people usually considered American heroes in order to back the argument that these heroes never would have been influenced by Indians. It is jarring to see enlightened modern scholars celebrate the bigotry of their heroes in order to stamp out scholarly inquiry with which they disagree. It is also telling that the leading gatekeepers of the Framers are white men, attacking scholars invoking (some merely mentioning it) the Haudenosaunee influence theory who are white women and people of color.

Third, and most importantly, the arguments against the Haudenosaunee influence theory highlight the blind spots in the history of the American founding: slavery and Indian killing. Federalism was the most efficient means by which the Framers could protect the evil institution of slavery, by limiting or even eradicating the power of the national government to rid America of slave-owning. States retained authority to decide whether slavery would be legal in their territories. Conversely, national power was the most efficient method to deal with Indian tribes. The Framers granted plenary and exclusive power to Congress to regulate commerce with Indian tribes. Even before there was a US Constitution, the United States had dealt with Indian tribes either through its war powers or treaty power; the Constitution changed nothing about that relationship.

If the Haudenosaunee influence theory really is hogwash, I'm personally glad. I'd hate for tribal constitutions to serve as a model for those slave-owning, Indian-hating white men who wrote the Constitution. The Constitution really was – and is – an incredibly efficient means for political elites to control people of color.

We should wish that Haudenosaunee political theory had more influence on the Framers than even Laura Nader claimed. The Haudenosaunee nations placed all the real political power with the clan mothers. Men did as they were told. Even today, Haudenosaunee people are not tribal citizens unless their mothers were tribal citizens. Those white men who framed and ratified the Constitution gave us slavery, Indian killing, dispossession of Indian lands, and the American Civil War. Even today, the white men who are in charge aren't doing much better.

Something tells me the influence thesis isn't going away anytime soon, no matter how angry scholars such as Gordon Wood get when someone that matters to them drops a footnote referencing it. The gatekeepers are completely tone deaf on this issue. How many other questions do gatekeepers stamp out?

The Anishinaabe giant, Mashos, met his match when he tried to murder his son-in-law. Mashos was sly and cunning. He pretended to warm to his son-in-law by inviting the young man on a series of adventures. He took the young man fishing for giant sturgeon, traveling an enormous distance by *jiimaan* (canoe) to a massive lake where the sturgeon lived. Then Mashos secretly called the sturgeon out to say he had brought a meal for the fish. While the young man slept in camp, Mashos sneaked away with the *jiimaan*. The young man avoided the attack of the sturgeon with guile and wisdom and eventually found his way home. Mashos was shocked, of course, having already explained that he saw the sturgeon monster consume the young man, but grudgingly welcomed his son-in-law home.

Mashos repeatedly took his son-in-law out for dangerous hunts, set up the young man for death, and sneaked back to the village. Each time, the young man barely avoided death and came back. Everyone knew Mashos was an attempted-murdering bastard, but the old man was so powerful, no one called him out.

Eventually, the young man got the better of Mashos on a dangerous trip to the highest mountain peak. The young man stole Mashos's moccasins and returned to the village while Mashos was tobogganing. Mashos had no shoes and couldn't return to his village. He froze to death on the mountain.

Gatekeepers like Mashos harm the community by quashing the ideas of the next generation. New ideas and methodologies disrupt the establishment. Whether those ideas prevail in the long run is a contest of ideas. But the younger generation always seems to get the upper hand eventually.

17

BABY STEALING (MODERN)

One of the more terrifying, yet compelling, stories told by Anishinaabe people is the story of the Old Toad-Woman who stole an Anishinaabe child.[259] The story begins with an idyllic Indian family living in the woods. A young man had married a young woman and built a lodge for her there, a little way off from the main community. Each day, he would leave to do his work, hunting and the like. And each day, she would handle her work, tending to the crops and the household. After a time, they conceived and she birthed a beautiful Benodjehn (child). Together, they designed and built a beautiful and intricate *tiginaagan* (cradleboard) for their child. All was well.

One day, when the young father was on a particularly long excursion, the young mother was alone with their Benodjehn. She had need of firewood, so she decided to leave the Benodjehn in the lodge while she gathered it. It was so difficult to carry both the rapidly growing child and the firewood. She wasn't gone long, but when she returned the Benodjehn was gone. She almost lost her mind, and rushed around the lodge searching for her child. She looked high and low, screaming for her baby. When the father returned, he looked, too. They searched and searched, and extended their search to the village where they grew up, asking everyone there if they had seen the Benodjehn. All efforts were for naught.

It turned out that Old Toad-Woman had been watching the young family. She was a greedy, jealous sort, homely and bitter. She lived alone even farther away from the village than the young couple, basically an outcast. Most people had even forgotten about her, she had been gone so long and had contributed so little to the village when she was there. When the young mother went to collect firewood, Old Toad-Woman seized the moment and sneaked stealthily into the lodge. She covered the Benodjehn's mouth with her gnarled and dirty old hands so he wouldn't cry out and stole that child. She moved quickly through the forest, carrying the beautiful *tiginaagan*, until she reached her own lodge. Her lodge was a messy affair, with dirt and debris everywhere, plus the leavings of her own children, the toad babies that she had birthed but did not love, and which inundated the lodge with their numbers.

Old Toad-Woman had desired a beautiful Benodjehn for her own gratification for many years. This young child fulfilled her twisted desires. She heaped praise and food on the Benodjehn, spoiling that baby rotten, all the while neglecting her own toad children. As the years passed, she taught everything she knew to the Benodjehn. And as he grew into a strong and swift Anishinaabe *inini* (man), he became a prodigious hunter. Every day, he would leave the lodge for the woods, and bring home a beaver, a deer, or even the occasional elk. And each day, Old Toad-Woman would hide, gut, and clean the animal, and smoke the extra meat for the winter. Old Toad-Woman's family lived well during those years.

But during that time, the young couple drifted apart. The husband never really forgave his wife for leaving their Benodjehn alone, even for a few minutes so she could gather wood. And she never really stopped looking for their child. The young man moved on, and she kept looking. She would never stop. As the years went by, the young woman still searched for her Benodjehn. She found little clues here and there in the woods. Tiny bits of birchbark that she believed could have been part of the *tiginaagan*. Or a piece of deer-hide leather that might have come from the *tiginaagan*. Over time, she began to realize that the little pieces of the *tiginaagan* might have come from her child's gnawing on it. She remembered that he was teething when he disappeared. She began to believe the tiny pieces of the *tiginaagan* formed a pattern where the baby thief had taken her child. She searched and searched.

Years passed and the young woman aged, but she never stopped search-ing. One day, she came to a small lodge far from her own lodge and vil-lage, much farther than she had ever searched before. She watched the lodge for a time, and envied the bounty it evidenced. The Anishinaabe people who lived there had fresh skins covering the lodge, multiple smoke houses circling the lodge indicating there was meat aplenty, and the whole area around the lodge was well kept and loved. It reminded her of her own lodge, before her Benodjehn had been taken, and it made her weep. Eventually, she saw the inhabitants of the lodge. In the morning, a young Anishinaabe *inini* clothed in the finest leather and moccasins left the lodge to go hunting. That young man looked remarkably like her own husband when he was a young man. It pained the woman to see the young man, and she began to wonder if he was her Benodjehn. As the young man prepared to leave, an elderly and decrepit woman came out of the lodge to wish him farewell. The watching woman had never seen Old Toad-Woman herself, but this homely creature fit the descriptions she had heard. The watching woman became convinced this was the Old Toad-Woman, that she had stolen her child and was now living her life. But she needed proof. The woman left for a time to formulate a plan to investigate this family. Af-ter the young man was out for some time, she wandered into the clearing where the lodge was and announced herself. "*Boozhoo!*" she called. The old woman came out, smiling, but smiling in a way the younger woman could never trust. "*Aaniin!*" the old woman said in response.

The younger woman explained that she had been searching for a lost child, not offering details, nor explaining how long she had been searching (it had been more than a decade). "There's not much of a trail," she said, "but it leads in this direction."

The Old Toad-Woman nodded, expressing false sympathy for the wom-an's plight. She had instantly recognized the younger woman, even though years had passed. This woman was going to be trouble. "I'm afraid you won't find anything here."

The younger woman remained deeply suspicious of the old woman. "That may true, but I think I'll stop here and rest, if you don't mind."

Old Toad-Woman minded greatly. "I'm afraid there's no room for anyone but me and my children in the lodge." She lifted aside the doorway to show off her home. It was spacious and beautiful, but it was indeed full of toad children.

"My, my," said the younger woman. "I wouldn't think of intruding anyway. I think I'll construct my own lodge a little way off. Stay out of your way. But I'll be around to help out, too, if you ever need anything. It'll be winter soon."

Old Toad-Woman didn't like that idea either, but as she was about to object, the young man returned home with yet another deer. He was a nice young man, warm and giving, and was delighted to have company. He liked the idea of the other woman moving in close by and even offered to help her build a lodge. Old Toad-Woman was stuck, and so she relented. The younger woman and the young man constructed a lodge. The young man shared some of their smoked meat and dried berries, and even their valuable deer and bear hides, all over the Old Toad-Woman's objections. The younger woman became more and more convinced that this handsome and generous young man was her own child. He was exactly what she had wanted her child to be, and he was exactly what her own husband had been like before their Benodjehn had been taken.

As winter approached, the younger woman brought the young man into her lodge. She asked some pointed questions. "How is it that Old Toad-Woman birthed you? All her other children are like her." The young man laughed off the questions, but a seed had been planted.

Time passed, and eventually the young man began to question Old Toad-Woman. He wasn't about to ask why he didn't look like his mother's other children, but he did have a question about the *tiginaagan*. "Why is my *tiginaagan* so much more intricate and strong than those for my brothers and sisters?" In the far corner of the lodge, the Old Toad-Woman kept the cradleboards for all her children. The ones for the toad children were pathetic compared to the young man's.

Old Toad-Woman was caught off guard by the question. "Have you been talking to that woman who lives a little way off?"

"Yes," the young man admitted. "What's wrong with that?"

"She is going to try to take you away from me," Old Toad-Woman said with hate and bile. "You should stay away from her."

The young man had seen his mother act mean, but never toward him. He was put off. "What about the *tiginaagan*?" he asked again.

Old Toad-Woman answered in that way that made her look like a liar. "Well, you were a precious child, weaker than my other children, and more beautiful, so I made you a better *tiginaagan*."

That sounded about right to the young man. He was better looking, but it seemed cold and callous as well.

The next day, the younger woman spoke again to the young man. "I once had a child who was taken from me. He would be about your age. His father helped me construct a *tiginaagan* from birchbark and the best leather we could make. I beaded the *ode'imin* (strawberry) on the *tiginaagan* to represent our love for our Benodjehn. And we painted our *dodem* (clan) on the back – *mai'ingan* (wolf) for his dad and *giigoon* (fish) for me."

The young man nodded as he listened.

The woman paused a moment. "I believe you are Neen Nghoos (my son). Go. Go look at the *tiginaagan*, and you will see." Before the young man left to investigate, the woman said one last thing. "You were teething when she took you. The bits of bark and leather that you chewed off the *tiginaagan* were how I found you."

The young man left and did discover the truth about the *tiginaagan*. He went hunting the next day, harvested two deer, and left them for the Old Toad-Woman. That night he left with his mother. They returned to the village and lived long lives.

It is the twenty-first century and Indian children are still being taken from their parents, both inside and outside of Indian country. All the statistics confirm that Indian children are removed from their homes at disproportionate rates by state governments. Poverty rates for Indian people on and off reservation are too often very high. Poverty leads to unemployment, drug and alcohol abuse, and poor health and dental care. The same is true for poor non-Indians as well. They are probably worse off because poor non-Indians don't have tribal governments to fall back on.

State and federal governments do pretty much nothing to prevent Americans from falling through the cracks and becoming poverty stricken. Most Americans, politically conservative and liberal both, support our economic and political system that creates winners and losers. Tribal governments tend to seek out preventative solutions, education, and jobs training, while state and federal governments simply don't.

What states and the federal government do, usually, is react to poverty rather than try to prevent it. Since the Great Depression, states and the federal government have paid vast sums to support a social safety net. There's nothing wrong with this system inherently. But it's wildly inefficient and, in the twenty-first century, wildly unpopular with many American voters.

In the context of child welfare, children in need of care because of parental abuse or neglect, states and the federal government do little to help families in need of assistance. Instead, they have set up a system that reacts by taking children in need of care away from their abusive or neglectful parents. To be sure, governments should remove children from physically abusive parents. But states also take kids away from loving parents with dirty homes, especially if the parents are people of color like Indian people.

The United States has created a market for children in need of care riddled with moral hazards. First, the federal government provides funding to states to pay for foster care. Instead of funding preventative measures that might more efficiently avert removals of children from their homes, states are encouraged by the availability of funds to remove children and place them in foster care. The federal money for foster care typically dries up after a year. Second, the federal government has enacted laws supporting private adoption of children removed from their homes. Because foster care funding typically disappears after a year, states are encouraged to place a time limit on parents whose kids they have taken to get their acts together – a year. That one year is a completely arbitrary period of time. Parents accused of neglect often need more than a year to recover from whatever caused their difficulties. After the year is over, the state actively seeks termination of parental rights. And the state actively seeks to find a permanent placement for children without parents, usually through adoption.

The private adoption market is a thing. Babies are priced by race and gender. Each adoption costs thousands in fees to the adoption agency, attorney fees, and court costs. Trade journals value the private adoption market at $16 billion and growing as federal funds for foster care disappear under Republican Party leadership in Washington, D.C. In 2016–2017, the average newborn adoption cost $43,000, with more than $18,000 of that amount going directly to adoption agencies. Children are assets to the private adoption market – lucrative assets.

Adoption is an important piece to the child welfare system, to be sure. Foster care by strangers is a terrible place for children to be. Children who age out of foster care having had none of the advantages of a loving, stable home typically have the worst outcomes. But adoption by strangers is only the best of the worst case scenarios, barely one better than aging out of foster care by strangers.

States started taking away Indian children en masse after the Great Depression. Some states began to believe as a matter of policy first, and then later law, that children living in Indian country were, by definition, children in need of care. Merely residing in poverty on Indian reservations, for many state agencies and workers, was the equivalent of child neglect, if not abuse. By the 1970s, the Association on American Indian Affairs reported that 25 to 35 percent of Indian children in the country had been removed from their Indian families, almost always to non-Indian placements.[260]

State workers and courts got the idea from the Bureau of Indian Affairs, which prototyped something called the Indian Adoption Project (IAP) in the early 1950s. Federal officials in the 1940s and 1950s were deeply engaged in the process of termination, the process of eliminating Indian affairs as a federal matter. They offered up Indian tribes to Congress as fodder for "termination," severing the federal–tribal trust relationship. The notion of termination infested federal officials' thinking. If the federal government was getting out of the Indian business, the thinking went, then they should encourage Indian people to get out of the business of being Indian. Federal money for Indian children's education and welfare was drying up, and state governments weren't stepping up to take on another unfunded mandate. Private adoption met several goals of these terminationist federal officials – primarily, killing the Indian to save the man. Adoption agencies favored white nuclear families as potential adoptive families. Federal officials favored eradicating Indian people. Hence, the IAP.

Over time, as the 1950s bled into the 1960s, for whatever reason or reasons, perhaps a function of American culture at that time, Indian children became incredibly valuable to the private adoption market. There was a great demand for Indian children. The IAP, which only ran for a few years and wound down after a few hundred adoptions, was a model for the mass removal of Indian children. The federal government showed how easy it was to snatch up Indian children and farm them out to non-Indian families. A few decades later, Indian children became hot commodities for white families. A literal asset.

The whole market for Indian babies became quite grotesque. Finally, in the 1970s, Indian mothers and grandmothers who had been demanding action for years got it when Congress began holding hearings on Indian child removals. Indian people made the compelling case that Indian tribes would eventually disappear if there were no children. Whole generations of Indian children had disappeared from their cultures, their traditions, their languages, their families, their communities. And outcomes for those kids who were removed were not good – suicide, alcohol and drug abuse, depression, crime, and so on were dramatically higher for Indian children removed to non-Indian homes either through adoption or foster care.

That was bad enough. Possibly what moved Congress of the 1970s to act was that Indian parents had no rights whatsoever in state courts. Imagine being an Indian parent, waiting for your children to come home from school, only to never see them again. Literally. Indian parents had no right to counsel, even if they could afford an attorney, which was rare. They had no right to contest the removal in state courts, no right to testify, to cross-examine witnesses, to present their own testimony. They usually were not even given notice. At times, state workers would show up at a reservation school with a bus and take as many Indian children as they could. They would quickly convene a hearing in state court (keep in mind that state officials often dispensed with a court hearing at all). State workers would testify to the judge that the child or children were in poverty, that they might be living with a grandparent, a cousin, or friend. State judges routinely granted the motion for an emergency removal, even without any evidence whatsoever that the children were in danger or in need of care. Indian families that appeared in court to contest the removal usually were not allowed to talk. They were not represented by counsel. They could not do much of anything to challenge the taking of their children by the state.

The federal government finally enacted the Indian Child Welfare Act (ICWA) in 1978. It guarantees the right to counsel,[261] the right to notice,[262] and the right to a hearing.[263] The state must notify the child's tribe, which can then intervene and even ask to move the case to tribal court,[264] a motion that state courts must grant unless the Indian child is not domiciled in Indian country *and* there is good cause not to transfer.[265] State courts cannot terminate the rights of Indian parents unless the state presents evidence beyond a reasonable doubt that there would be serious emotional or physical damage to the child.[266]

The legislative history of the act shows that the loudest opposition to the law came from the private adoption market, both secular and religious. The religious adoption agencies and the secular adoption agencies complained that the law would slow down, even prevent, private adoptions of Indian children. Of course, that was the whole point. But even to the religious adoption agencies, and certainly to private adoption agencies, Indian children were assets. Perhaps the private adoption market wasn't in the tens of billions of dollars like it is today, but the market was definitely lucrative then as well. So the private adoption market proxies came out in force against any bill attempting to protect Indian children from that market.

Regardless, Congress passed ICWA by voice vote, with no public opposition from America's elected representatives. Cribbing from the Casey Family Programs brief in *Adoptive Couple v. Baby Girl*, a Supreme Court decision addressing an aspect of the statute, ICWA should be considered the "gold standard" of child welfare codes nationally.[267] Compared to the state law regimes predating ICWA, which offered little or no due process to any parents, ICWA dramatically heightened the rights of parents. Fast forward four decades, and ICWA continues to inspire reforms to child welfare laws nationally. Some states have even adopted large chunks of ICWA for all children and parents. Child welfare is broken in far too many states and jurisdictions, but ICWA is a model for reform.

In 2020, the same moneyed interests that opposed ICWA in the 1970s still opposed it – the private adoption market. The industry's opposition is spearheaded by conservative legal reform groups that claim Indian children are penalized by ICWA, which denies them access to state foster care services and by extension the private adoption market. It's kind of like saying child labor laws prevent children from accessing the dangerous manufacturing sector by making kids go to school instead.

The core of the substantive argument against ICWA is an old one – growing up Indian is bad. Mark Fiddler, an Indian lawyer who advocates against Indian tribes in Indian child welfare cases, has asserted that his goal is to get as many Indian children into foster care as possible, a statement that makes rational child welfare professionals worry for his sanity – and his Indian child clients. But it's a perfectly sane and rational position to take, at least for Indian-haters who have a financial interest in the foster care and private adoption market.

There's more, because there always is, and when it comes to Indian-hating, it always gets worse. As mentioned, an adoption cost $43,000 on average in 2016–2017. Details on specific adoptions are sketchy, but there is an enormous amount of anecdotal evidence that the market prices babies by race and gender. Babies of African-American descent are priced downward, perhaps because of the figurative price that every Black person pays to be Black in America. The same appears to be true of Latinx and Asian babies. One would think it is also true of Indian babies. Or is it? Imagine an Indian baby on the private adoption market who stands to receive an entitlement from their tribe when they become adults, perhaps a per capita payment arising from a trust fund account set aside by their tribe. One would think the price on the private adoption market for that Indian baby could rise dramatically. That's how the private adoption market works. There is a price tag on Indian babies.

Twenty-first century Indian tribes are entering their fifth and sixth decades of self-determination, an era that began in the 1970s. They have control over their own government services. They spend, per capita, more on child welfare and other children's services than states or the federal government. They are not influenced by moneyed interests like the private adoption market. Their children are assets, but not financial assets – they are cultural building blocks of an Indian tribe's future.

The theft of Indian babies is an ancient tradition that continues today. The story of Old Toad-Woman is a story about how some people think of Indian children as assets. Old Toad-Woman profited materially from stealing an Indian baby. That Anishinaabe *inini* she stole as a child hunted for her, providing the raw materials for food and shelter, helped to maintain her lodge, and effectively made her wealthy.

Compare Toad-Woman to the mother in the story, who relentlessly searched for her child. The Anishinaabe mother had already lost everything but continued to search for her lost bird. She never gave up, and in the end she found her child. She brought her baby home.

American Indian tribes are doing the same thing. They are doing their best to create a safe space for their children. Anishinaabe people would have it no other way.

CONCLUSION

One the scariest stories told by the Anishinaabeg is the story of the orphans, sometimes known as the story of the magic flight.[268] In this story, there is a lodge with a father, a mother, and two children, one of them an infant still in a cradleboard. Each day, the father leaves the lodge to hunt and gather, doing manly things. In one version of the story, the mother stops feeding the husband when he comes home. She has enough supplies to feed the whole family, but tells the older child to lie to the father about the food. So he gets used to going hungry. Eventually, the child tells the father that there's plenty of food, and the mother doesn't want to feed the father. In another version of the story, the mother isn't feeding the family much at all. No one is thriving. In both versions, during the day, right after the father leaves for work, the mother leaves the lodge. She is having an affair with a serpent. One day, after he realizes something is wrong, the father pretends to leave the lodge in the morning. Instead, he hides. He sees the mother leave the lodge and clandestinely follows her. He discovers the mother's secret. He returns to the lodge. He tells the eldest child to pack a bag, carry the baby, and leave the lodge, heading out into the winter. He instructs the child, "Walk in this direction until you come to the next lodge. Nokomis, a grandmother, will be there and will help you. Whatever you do," the father instructs, "no matter what you hear, *don't look back*." The father sends the eldest child, carrying the baby in the cradleboard, out the doorway of the lodge. The father kills the mother upon her return. The orphans walk on into the snow, into the darkness. After a time, the elder child hears the mother's voice. "Come home," the ghostly voice of their mother speaks. "Come back to me. I love you. I must suckle my baby." The elder child heeds the warning and instruction of the father, and refuses to turn and look. But the mother's ghost is always right behind, alternately sad, angry, loving, whatever might work to persuade the child to turn around and give in to the mother. Eventually, the children reach the lodge. There is a grandmother there who brings them in, feeds them, shelters them, lets them rest. But after a time, the grandmother tells the children that they must leave again. *Nokomis* helps the child with a new pack and helps load up the cradleboard. "Now walk out in the same direction, and whatever you do, don't look back." The oldest child trudges out into the night and again hears the mother plead with them to return to her. The children walk and walk until they reach another lodge. *Mishomis*, a grandfather, opens his lodge to the orphans. They stay, they rest, they are fed, but *mishomis* makes them leave again. The children again enter the dark winter, and again hear their mother. This process repeats again and again. In some versions, the children are always walking away from their mother's ghost. Sometimes the oldest child uses magic items to create magical barriers that slow down the mother's ghost, but the magic never holds her back for long. In some versions, this process never ends. In other versions, the orphans don't lose the ghostly mother until they pass over a river, which seems a lot like the river of the dead in other stories. In still other versions, the eldest orphan finally gives up and turns around to face the mother, with enormous consequences.

I think this is a story about grief, and about moving on from past horrors. For too many Indian people, past tragedies filter into contemporary lives. There is repetition to those stories, to these tragedies. This book is divided into two main sections, ancient and modern Indian-hating. The older examples of Indian-hating are bad enough. The modern examples, readers hopefully have concluded by now, are often simple repetitions of the older examples of Indian-hating. The same stories are played out again and again. Indian-hating in America is dense, it is broad, it is pervasive, and it is subtle. Indian-hating is disguised and it is covert. But at times it is also overt and often arrogantly so. And it follows Indian people around like ghosts. It shows up all over the place, in expected and unexpected places, and it is all but impossible to avoid.

Like the orphans, Indian people could be said to have a choice. We can keep moving forward, holding back the forms of Indian-hating that follow us around like ghosts. We can try to forget, to form new memories, to make new decisions, new lives, to defeat Indian-hating by forging a better life. There will be people on the path ahead, like the *nokomis* and *mishomis* figures in the story, who can help. There will be tools along the path that can help, too. This is a path of always moving forward. That's a path to which I believe my own personality is best suited. But there are costs to that path. Never turning to address the source of trauma can be counterproductive. The orphans' path never seems to end, no matter how tired, hungry, and cold they get. They also never really seem to grow up.

Alternatively, Indian people can turn and face the trauma. There are several alternate versions of what happens to the orphans in the end when they finally turn to face the mother. In some versions, the ghost takes the baby in the cradleboard, and that baby is lost forever. The eldest child grows up, traumatized, always knowing what happened, but lives to adulthood, makes a new life, moves forward. In other versions, the baby taken by the mother turns into a wolf. After this trauma, the wolf goes to live in the area where the eldest child lives so it can watch over the child. In some of the most obscure versions, the orphans survive the mother's ghost, thanks to the intervention of adults, or the *manidowaag* (spirits). Similarly, some Indian people who turn to face the trauma become lost in it. Others are damaged, but survive. Happy ending or no, there are always consequences, good and bad.

Tribal organizations, including governments, schools, programs, businesses, and so on, don't have emotions. They are just entities, paper entities even, created and managed on literal pieces of paper (or figurative digital code). But at least in recent decades, they are paper entities created and shaped by Indian people. Indian people bring their own experiences and cultural guideposts to operating and governing these paper organizations. Organizations are best suited to moving on, not looking back, carving new histories in the face of ancient and modern Indian-hating. Weirdly, for many

Indian people, including myself, these paper organizations are a lot like a lifeboat. Tribes are timeless entities. They are paper organizations with legal, economic, and political status in the United States. They are flawed, sometimes deeply flawed, entities, managed by traumatized victims and survivors of Indian-hating past and present. They sometimes do horrible things, at the bidding of Indian people (and often by non-Indian people). But usually they do good things, and have the potential to do great things. They belong to Indian people. Most importantly, while Indian people come and go, tribal nations aren't going to disappear.

There's one last version of the story of the orphans that only makes sense to me now that I write these final sentences. In that story, the orphans turn and confront their mother, the ghost that follows them.[269] The baby is transformed into a wolf. The elder child is rescued and goes to live with the family of the giant named Mashos. There are lots of stories about this giant Mashos, too, but they are usually presented as stand-alone stories. In the Mashos stories, the giant is always trying to kill his son-in-law by taking him somewhere on a hunt and leaving him to be consumed by a monster or destroyed by the elements.[270] But the son-in-law always survives by guile and wit, and eventually Mashos himself is left out in the cold and succumbs, a victim of his own vicious trickery. In this version of the story, that elder orphan is the focus of two enormous adventures. The first is a story of tremendous horror and grief, and the second is a story of survival and resilience. Some Anishinaabe storyteller thought it was a good idea to combine these two stories, thereby transforming them into a saga, a saga beginning with horror but then moving toward a courageous victory, a saga that Indian people long have been living.

POSTLUDE FOR OWEN AND EMMETT

In line with this project on Indian-hating is one my personal favorite stories, a story that is not a traditional Anishinaabe story, not an Indian story at all. This one is for my sons, Owen and Emmett Singel-Fletcher. It's a story about something called "the vault" from a pair of linked episodes of the cartoon show *Adventure Time*. The show is about a little boy and his talking magical dog, set a thousand years into a postapocalyptic future. Amazing and terrifying adventures happen all the time. On several occasions throughout the show, *Adventure Time* characters show signs of mental distress. For example, when a character from the Cloud Kingdom named Carol yells out loud suddenly, she explains, "I just thought about my anxieties, and it's like my mind hand touched a hot memory stove."[271] I think a lot of Indian people can relate.

Adventure Time's main character, known as Finn the Human, is just a little boy. He ages during the decade the show was on TV, from a small boy into a young man. In the episode titled "The Vault,"[272] Finn is having nightmares, sleepwalking, and wrecking furniture in the house he shares with Jake the Dog, who is a magical talking dog. When Jake confronts Finn about the nightmares, Finn refuses to talk about his dreams. He confesses that he puts memories he can't handle in a part of his mind he calls the "vault," and he would rather not open the vault. In fact, he would pretty much do anything he can to avoid opening the vault. He reasons that he's not really hurting anyone, so it's no big deal. Yet he's wrecking the house each time he sleepwalks during one of his nightmares.

In a previous episode, titled "The Creeps,"[273] Finn saw something he couldn't handle, a horrifying ghost. At that time, he said to himself, "That's going in the vault." He then tapped his noggin, adding, "Aaaaand it's g. . . ." That episode ended abruptly as Finn repressed his memory about the terrifying ghost. In "The Vault" episode, Jake eventually tricks Finn into confronting his repressed memories – opening the vault. Inside the vault, Finn realizes that in a previous life hundreds of years ago, he was a girl named Shoko. Shoko stole a magic "omelet" (amulet) from his friend Princess Bubblegum (who is secretly hundreds of years old but passes for eighteen). Finn subconsciously feels guilty about Shoko's theft of the amulet, although he only learned about it from his nightmares. Shoko is the terrifying ghost he saw in "The Creeps" and who Finn is now seeing in his nightmare. Finn is the thief and the ghost he sees in his nightmares. Finn finds the stolen amulet buried underneath his house and returns it to Princess Bubblegum. The episode ends with Finn saying, "Huh. My vault feels lighter."

After completing this project, so does mine.

Miigwetch.

ACKNOWLEDGMENTS

Miigwetch to my immediate family, Wenona T. Singel, Owen W. Singel-Fletcher, Emmett W. Singel-Fletcher, June Mamagona Fletcher, Zeke Fletcher, the nephews, niece, cousins, and in-laws, the dog, and those who have walked on.

Special thanks to John Borrows, Kristen Carpenter, John-Paul Chalykoff, Tiffani Darden, Sam Deloria, Kate Fort, Eric Hemenway, Reagyn Germer, Brian Gilmore, Catherine Grosso, Myriam Jaïdi, Tiya Miles, Doreen McPaul, Monte Mills, Dylan Miner, Meg Noodin, Dr. Barbara O'Brien, Migizi Pensoneau, Emma Petoskey, Eva Petoskey, John Petoskey, Johnny Petoskey, Michael Petoskey, Rose Petoskey, Emily Proctor, Angela Riley, Dr. Nick Reo, Neoshia Roemer, Kaighn Smith, Paul Stebleton, David Thronson, Veronica Thronson, Estrella Torrez, Brian Upton, Kyle Whyte, Monica Williamson, Novaline Wilson, April Youpee-Roll, all the students, alumni, and supporters of the Indigenous Law and Policy Center, the Friday Forum, the QuaranTICA crew, and the Quarantiki crew. Thanks to Walter Echo-Hawk for the kindness and generosity to introduce me to the team at Fulcrum Publishing. Thanks to Alison Auch, my editor.

Finally, thanks to American Indian and Indigenous Studies at Michigan State University, Anishinaabe Racial Justice Conference, Dartmouth College, Society for the Study of Midwestern Literature, and Western Michigan University for giving me space to talk about the ideas in this book.

REFERENCES

1. Nanaboozhoo is the shapeshifting trickster-god of Anishinaabe lore. He was born a rabbit (*wabooz*), so many stories say his original name was Chi-Wa-booz or Mishabooz – "big bunny." There are so many spellings of his name – Manabazo, Nanapush, Wenabozho, and so many others. I prefer Nanaboozhoo, because it is so ridiculously wrong I imagine the big bunny would think it was funny.

2. Anishinaabe, or Anishinaabeg or Anishinabek in plural form, is a preferred spelling of the Indian people of the western Great Lakes and beyond, the Odawa (Ottawa), Ojibwe or Ojibwa (Chippewa), and Bodewadmi (Potawatomi) tribal nations.

3. More Adventures of Manabazoo, in Beatrice Blackwood, *Tales of the Chippewa Indians*, 40: 4 Folklore 316, 329–332 (1929).

4. Herman Melville, Containing the Metaphysics of Indian-hating, According to the Views of One Evidently Not So Prepossessed as Rousseau in Favor of Savages, in *The Confidence Man* (1857).

5. Cormac McCarthy, *Blood Meridian or The Evening Redness in the West* (1985).

6. Leslie Marmon Silko, *Indian Hater, Indian Fighter, Indian Killer: Melville's Indictment of the "New Nation" and the "New World,"* 14:1 Leviathan 94 (2012).

7.   Eva Petoskey, 40 Years of the Indian Civil Rights Act: Indigenous Women's Reflections, in *The Indian Civil Rights Act at Forty* 39, 47–48 (Kristen A. Carpenter, Matthew L. M. Fletcher, and Angela R. Riley, eds. 2012) (quoting Eva Petoskey, Address, Michigan State University College of Law, Indigenous Law and Policy Center, 5th Annual Indigenous Law Conference (Oct. 10–11, 2008)).

8.   Fred Kelly, Anishinaabe Leadership, at 3 (Dec. 14, 2005), quoted in Vanessa A. Watts, Towards Anishinaabe Governance and Accountability: Reawakening our Relationships and Sacred Bimaadziwin 77, unpublished master's thesis, University of Victoria (2006).

9.   Edward Benton-Benai, *The Mishomis Book: The Voice of the Ojibway* 64 (1979) (emphasis in original).

10.   E.g., Lawrence W. Gross, *Bimaadiziwin, or the "Good Life," as a Unifying Concept of Anishinaabe Religion*, 26:1 Am. Indian Culture & Res. J. 15, 26 (2002).

11.   E.g., Jaro Kotalik and Gerry Martin, *Aboriginal Health Care and Bioethics: A Reflection on the Teaching of the Seven Grandfathers*, 16:5 Am. J. Bioethics 38 (2016).

12.   E.g., David B. Anderson, *Preparing to Teach Our Children the Foundations for an Anishinaabe Curriculum*, 37:3 McGill J. Educ. 293 (2002).

13.   E.g., Deborah McGregor, *Coming Full Circle: Indigenous Knowledge, Environment, and Our Future*, 28:3/4 Am. Indian Q. 385, 404 (2004).

14.   E.g., Margaret Noodin, *Bawaajimo: A Dialect of Dreams in Anishinaabe Language and Literature* 138–145 (2014).

15.   John Borrows, *Seven Gifts: Revitalizing Living Laws Through Indigenous Legal Practice*, 2:1 Lakehead L.J. 2, 3 (2016–2017) ("Anishinaabe law speaks about applying the seven grandfather/grandmother teachings: we must learn to treat each other with wisdom, respect, love, bravery, truth, humility, and honesty.").

16.   Mark. F. Ruml, *The Indigenous Knowledge Documentation Project – Morrison Sessions: Gagige Inaakonige, The Eternal Natural Laws*, 30:2 Religious Studies and Theology 155, 163 (2011).

17.   Ruml, *supra* at 166.

18. Lindsay Keegitah Borrows, *Otter's Journey through Indigenous Language and Law* (2018).

19. The Birth of Nanabushu, in 1 William Jones, *Ojibwa Texts* 3–7 (Truman Michelson ed. 1917). See also A. F. Chamberlain, *Nanibozhu amongst the Otchipwe, Mississagas, and Other Algonkian Tribes*, 4:14 J. Am. Folklore 193 (1891).

20. Edward Benton-Benai, *The Mishomis Book: The Voice of the Ojibway* 95–103 (1979).

21. Benton-Benai, *supra* at 30–35; Beatrice Blackwood, *Tales of the Chippewa Indians*, 40:4 Folklore 315, 323–328 (1929).

22. Richard Delgado, *The Imperial Scholar: Reflections on a Review of Civil Rights Literature*, 132 U. Pa. L. Rev. 561, 565 (1984).

23. I was once told in law school that legal scholarship on federal Indian law authored by an Indian person was inherently biased and would be suspect.

24. Elena Kagan, Hearing before the Senate Committee on the Judiciary (June 29, 2010).

25. Richard Epstein, *Common Law, Labor Law, and Reality: A Rejoinder to Professors Getman and Kohler*, 92 Yale Law Journal 1435, 1435 (1983).

26. 554 U.S. 570 (2008).

27. See generally Angela R. Riley, *Indians and Guns*, 100 Geo. L.J. 1675 (2012).

28. See Chapter 2.

29. Ann Tweedy's article on the subject of guns in Indian Country quotes a question from Justice Kennedy in the *Heller* argument. Ann E. Tweedy, *"Hostile Indian Tribes . . . Outlaws, Wolves, . . . Bears . . . Grizzlies and Things like That?" How the Second Amendment and Supreme Court Precedent Target Tribal Self-Defense*, 13 U. Pa. J. Const. L. 687 (2011).

30. Treaty of Fort Pitt with the Delaware Nation, Sept. 17, 1778, 7 Stat. 13.

31. Matthew L. M. Fletcher, *Federal Indian Law* § 2.3, at 37–39 (2016) (1763 British Proclamation); *id.* § 3.1, at 51–53 (Trade and Intercourse Act of 1790).

32. Eric A. Kades, *The Dark Side of Efficiency:* Johnson v. M'Intosh *and the Expropriation of Amerindian Lands*, 148 U. Pa. L. Rev. 1065 (2000); Terry

L. Anderson and Fred S. McChesney, *Raid or Trade? An Economic Model of Indian-White Relations*, 37 J. L. & Econ. 39 (1994).

33. Colin G. Calloway, *The Victory with No Name: The Native American Defeat of the First American Army* (2015).

34. *Kennedy v. Louisiana*, 554 U.S. 407 (2008) (Kennedy, J.).

35. Brief for Amicus Curiae the President Pro Tempore of the Senate of Pennsylvania, Joseph B. Scarnati, III, in Support of Respondent, *District of Columbia v. Heller*, 554 U.S. 570 (2008) (No. 07-290), 2008 WL 405573.

36. Harry G. Frankfurt, *On Bullshit* (2005 reprint).

37. Pub. L. 90–284, Title II, § 201, 82 Stat. 77 (1968), codified at 25 U.S.C. § 1302(a).

38. James D. Diamond, *After the Bloodbath: Is Healing Possible in the Wake of Rampage Shootings?* (2019).

39. Snapping-Turtle and the Cadice-Fly, Snapping-Turtle Goes to War, and Snapping-Turtle Goes to War, in 2 William Jones, *Ojibwa Texts* 107–113, 113–121, 339–349 (Truman Michelson ed. 1919).

40. Lewis Cass, *British Policy in Respect to the Indians* (January 1840), reprinted in Special Heritage Issue: The Indian Question, 1823–1973, 258:4 North American Review 24–25 (Winter 1973).

41. Matthew L. M. Fletcher, *Federal Indian Law* § 3.2, at 53–56 (2016).

42. Treaty of Washington, 7 Stat. 491 (1836).

43. Matthew L. M. Fletcher, *The Eagle Returns: The Legal History of the Grand Traverse Band of Ottawa and Chippewa Indians*, ch. 1, at 1–35 (2012).

44. "We feel such an attachment to this our native place, from whence we derive our birth, that it looks like going to certain death from it." Fletcher, *The Eagle Returns, supra* at 38.

45. Turtle's War-Party, in Alanson Skinner, *Plains Ojibwa Tales*, 32:124 J. Am. Folklore 280, 295–297 (1919).

46. Basil Johnston, Nana'b'oozoo and the Skunk, in *Living in Harmony* (Mino-nawae-indawewin) (2011).

47.   The story of the Osage Nation's mineral wealth and the subsequent "Reign of Terror" is told in Dennis McAuliffe, Jr., *Bloodland: A Family Story of Oil, Greed and Murder on the Osage Reservation* (1994), and David Grann, *Killers of the Flower Moon: The Osage Murders and the Birth of the FBA* (2017).

48.   Letter from H. S. Taylor to Commissioner of Indian Affairs, quoted in Partition of the Surface Rights of Navajo-Hopi Indian Land, Hearings before the Subcommittee on Indian Affairs, Committee on Interior and Insular Affairs, United States Senate, 93d Cong., 1st Sess. (Mar. 7, 1973).

49.   Letter from H. S. Traylor to Commissioner of Indian Affairs, reprinted in Indian Appropriation Bill, 1920, Hearings before the Committee on Indian Affairs, United States Senate, 65th Cong. 3d Sess. at 397, 403 (1919) [Traylor Potawatomi Report].

50.   Letter from H. S. Traylor to Commissioner of Indian Affairs, reprinted in Osage Extension, Hearings before the Committee on Indian Affairs, United States Senate, 66th Cong., 3d Sess. at 83 (1920) [Traylor Osage Report].

51.   Traylor Osage Report, *supra* at 83.

52.   Traylor Osage Report, *supra* at 83–84.

53.   Traylor Osage Report, *supra* at 85.

54.   Traylor Osage Report, *supra* at 86.

55.   Traylor Osage Report, *supra* at 87.

56.   Traylor Osage Report, *supra* at 89.

57.   The Thunder-Birds and the Water-Imps, in William Jones, *Ojibwa Tales from the North Shore of Lake Superior*, 29 J. Am. Folklore 368, 383–384 (1916).

58.   Colin G. Calloway, *The Victory with No Name: The Native American Defeat of the First American Army* (2015).

59.   Annual Report of the Commissioner of Indian Affairs – The Year 1848, Exec. Doc. 1 (November 30, 1846) [Medill Report].

60.   Medill Report, *supra* at 385.

61.   Medill Report, *supra* at 385.

62.   Medill Report, *supra* at 385.

63.   Medill Report, *supra* at 386.

64.   Medill Report, *supra* at 386.

65.   Medill Report, *supra* at 386.

66.   Medill Report, *supra* at 386.

67.   Medill Report, *supra* at 386.

68.   See Chapter 7.

69.   E.g., Colin G. Calloway, *The Indian History of an American Institution: Native Americans and Dartmouth* (2010).

70.   Adventures of Nanaboozhoo – IV, V, and VI, in William Jones, *Ojibwa Tales from the North Shore of Lake Superior*, 29 J. Am. Folklore 368, 390–391 (1916); Manabozho Goes Visiting, in Paul Radin and A. B. Reagan, *Ojibwa Myths and Tales: The Manabozho Cycle*, 14 J. Am. Folklore 61, 77–84 (Jan.–Mar. 1928).

71.   See Chapter 2.

72.   Matthew L. M. Fletcher, *Federal Indian Law* § 3.6, at 69–74 (2016).

73.   Merrill Gates, Opening Address, 18 *Proceedings of the Annual Meeting of the Lake Mohonk Conference Of The Friends Of The Indian* 10, 16 (1901).

74.   Gates, *supra* at 10.

75.   Gates, *supra* at 13.

76.   16 Stat. 566, codified at 25 U.S.C. § 71.

77.   Gates, *supra* at 14.

78.   Gates, *supra* at 14.

79.   Helen Hunt Jackson, *A Century of Dishonor* (1881).

80.   Charles F. Wilkinson, *American Indians, Time, and the Law* 14 (1987).

81.   Gates, *supra* at 16.

82.   Gates, *supra* at 16.

83.   See Chapter 7.

84.   Treaty of Detroit, 11 Stat. 621 (1855).

85. Treaty of Washington, 7 Stat. 491 (1836).

86. Fletcher, *supra* § 12.2, at 511–516.

87. The Jeebi; or, Two Ghosts, in Henry Schoolcraft, *The Myth of Hiawatha, and Other Oral Legends* 81–85 (1856).

88. Matthew L. M. Fletcher, *Federal Indian Law* § 3.7, at 84–85 (2016).

89. 12 Stat. 945 (1855).

90. *United States v. Clapox*, 35 F. 575 (D. Or. 1888).

91. Rose Stremlau, *To Domesticate and Civilize Wild Indians: Allotment and the Campaign to Reform Indian Families, 1875–1887*, 30 J. Fam. Hist. 265, 266 (2005).

92. *Clapox*, 35 F. at 576.

93. Pub. L. 103–141, Nov. 16, 1993, 107 Stat. 1488, codified at 42 U.S.C. §§ 2000bb et seq.

94. T. W. Davenport, *Recollections of an Indian Agent*, 8:1 Quarterly of the Oregon Historical Soc'y 1, 18 (Mar. 1907).

95. *United States v. Kagama*, 118 U.S. 375 (1886).

96. Act of Mar. 3, 1885, ch. 341, 23 Stat. 385, codified as amended at 18 U.S.C. § 1153.

97. An act to regulate trade and intercourse with the Indian tribes, July 22, 1790, 1 Stat. 137, now codified as amended at 25 U.S.C. §§ 177, 261–265; 18 U.S.C. § 1152.

98. *Kagama*, 118 U.S. at 385, quoted in *Clapox*, 35 F. at 577.

99. *Kagama*, 118 U.S. at 383–384.

100. Andrés Reséndes, *The Other Slavery: The Uncovered Story of Indian Enslavement in America* (2016).

101. Robert F. Hezier, *The Eighteen Unratified Treaties of 1851–1852 between the California Indians and the United States Government* (1972).

102. Treaty of Walla Walla, *supra* art. VIII.

103. *Clapox*, 35 F. at 577.

104. *Clapox*, 35 F. at 576.

105. *Clapox*, 35 F. at 577.

106 *Clapox*, 35 F. at 577.

107. See Chapter 7.

108. *Clapox*, 35 F. at 579.

109. *Clapox*, 35 F. at 578.

110. *Clapox*, 35 F. at 579.

111. Pub. L. 113–4, Title IX, § 904, Mar. 7, 2013, 127 Stat. 120, codified in relevant part at 25 U.S.C. § 1304.

112. The Flight of "Rising Sun," in John C. Wright, *The Crooked Tree* 91–98 (1915); Journey to the Spirit-World, in 2 William Jones, *Ojibwa Texts* 3–23 (Truman Michelson, ed. 1919).

113. Thomas J. Morgan, *A Plea for the Papoose*, reprinted at 18:12 Baptist Home Mission Monthly, Dec. 1896, at 402–410.

114. Morgan, *supra* at 403.

115. Morgan, *supra* at 403.

116. Morgan, *supra* at 404.

117. Morgan, *supra* at 408.

118. Morgan, *supra* at 408.

119. Nanabozho and Paul Bunyan, in Sister Bernard Coleman, Ellen Frogner, and Estelle Rich, *Ojibwa Myths and Legends* 99 (1962); Mary Siisip Geniusz, *Plants Have So Much to Give Us, All We Have to Do Is Ask: Anishinaabe Botanical Teachings* 81–82 (2015).

120. First Treaty of Fort Laramie, 11 Stat. 749 (1851); Second Treaty of Fort Laramie, 15 Stat. 649 (1868).

121. Waganakising Odawa Nation (Little Traverse Bay Bands of Odawa Indians), Constitution (2005).

122. Jeremy Waldron, *Superseding Historic Injustice*, 103:1 Ethics 4 (1992).

123. The fee to trust process is authorized and codified at 25 U.S.C. § 5108 and 25 C.F.R. Parts 151 and 292. The United States also authorized the secretary of the interior to acquire land in trust in numerous tribe-specific statutes, such as the Pokagon Band Restoration Act, Pub. L. 103–323, Sept. 21, 1994, 108 Stat. 2153.

124. See Chapter 9.

125. *United States v. Sioux Nation of Indians*, 448 U.S. 371 (1980).

126. Vine Deloria, Jr., *The Metaphysics of Modern Existence* (1979).

127. The Departure of Manabozho, in Alden O. Deming, *Manabozho: The Indian Story of Hiawatha* 82–87 (1838). Deming claimed to have retold tales collected by Schoolcraft. *Id.* at vi.

128. Raymond Kiogima, Legend of the Bear Walk, in Andrew J. Blackbird and Raymond Kiogima, *Odawa Language and Legends* 221–225 (2006); Bearwalkers, in Richard M. Dorson, *Bloodstoppers and Bearwalkers: Folk Traditions of the Upper Peninsula* 26–37 (1952).

129. See Chapter 1.

130. Naomi Schaefer Riley, *The New Trail of Tears: How Washington Is Destroying American Indians* (2016).

131. See Chapters 5 and 6.

132. Schaefer Riley, *supra* at 66.

133. Schaefer Riley, *supra* at 66.

134. Schaefer Riley, *supra* at 6.

135. Derek Brouwer, *Ending Decade of Litigation, Tribe and Catholic School Reach Settlement over Exploitation Suit*, Billings Gazette, Jan. 18, 2015.

136. Schaefer Riley, *supra* at 6.

137. Schaefer Riley, *supra* at 6.

138. Schaefer Riley, *supra* at 7.

139. Schaefer Riley, *supra* at 75.

140. *United States v. Chavis*, No. 4:17-cr-00134-HSG (N.D. Cal.).

141. National Public Radio, Former Educator Embraces "Crazy" Teaching Style, Sept. 8, 2009.

142. Schaefer Riley, *supra* at 107.

143. Felix M. Bordewich, *Killing the White Man's Indian: Reinventing Native Americans at the End of the Twentieth Century* (1996).

144. Elizabeth Cook-Lyn, *Book Review*, 12:1 Wíčazo Ša Rev. 228, 228 (1997).

145. Schaefer Riley, *supra* at 68.

146. Schaefer Riley, *supra* at 68.

147. Malinda Maynor Lowery, *Lumbee Indians in the Jim Crow South: Race, Identity, and the Making of a Nation* (2010).

148. Schaefer Riley, *supra* at 69.

149. Schafer Riley, *supra* at 70.

150. Schafer Riley, *supra* at 72.

151. Robert J. Miller and Maril Hazlett, *The Drunken Indian: Myth Distilled into Reality through Federal Indian Alcohol Policy*, 28 Ariz. St. L.J. 223 (1996).

152. Schaefer Riley, *supra* at 75.

153. Schafer Riley, *supra* at 118–119.

154. Schafer Riley, *supra* at 48.

155. Schaefer Riley, *supra* at 48.

156. Schaefer Riley, *supra* at 60.

157. Schaefer Riley, *supra* at 96.

158. Schaefer Riley, *supra* at 62.

159. Schaefer Riley, *supra* at 62, 63.

160. Schaefer Riley, *supra* at 63. Israel might be an interesting comparison for tribal governments. Like Israel, which perhaps might not exist in its current form without American resources and protection, many Indian nations are heavily dependent on appropriations and technical assistance from the United States. Like Israel, where 70 percent or more of its land is owned by the government, most of the land in Indian Country is controlled by federal or tribal governments.

161. Schaefer Riley, *supra* at 64.

162. Schaefer Riley, *supra* at 65.

163. Schaefer Riley, *supra* at 65–66.

164. Pub. L. 93–638, Jan. 4, 1975, 88 Stat. 2203, codified as amended at 25 U.S.C. § 5301 et seq.

165. Schaefer Riley, *supra* at 167.

166. Schaefer Riley, *supra* at 167.

167. Ian Haney López, *Dog Whistle Politics* (2014).

168. Matthew L. M. Fletcher, *The Eagle Returns: The Legal History of the Grand Traverse Band of Ottawa and Chippewa Indians* (2012); James M. McClurken, *Our People, Our Journey: The Little River Band of Ottawa Indians* (2009); James M. McClurken, *Gah-baeh-Jhagwah-buk: A Visual Culture History of the Little Traverse Bay Bands of Odawa* (1991).

169. Native American Oral History Project, *The Tree That Never Dies: Oral History of the Michigan Indians* 127 (Grand Rapids Public Library 1978).

170. Cheryl I. Harris, *Whiteness as Property*, 106 Harv. L. Rev. 1707 (1993).

171. *Little Traverse Bay Bands of Odawa Indians v. Whitmer*, 398 F.Supp.3d 201 (W.D. Mich. 2019), appeal filed Sept. 26, 2019 (6th Cir.) (No. 19-2070).

172. Treaty of Washington, 7 Stat. 491 (1836); Treaty of Detroit, 11 Stat. 621 (1855).

173. Emmet County Lakeshore Association, Protection of Rights Alliance, Tribe's Lawsuit Threatens Northern Michigan Way of Life and Property Values: The Time for Action Is Now! (Aug. 19, 2016).

174. "Indian country" is a legal term of art defined in 18 U.S.C. § 1151.

175. Pub. L. 95–608, Nov. 8, 1978, 92 Stat. 3069, codified at 25 U.S.C. § 1901 et seq.

176. John Cappa, The Wolf's Way, in Mary Magoulick, *Telling New Myths: Contemporary Native American Animal Narratives from Michigan*, 130 J. of Am. Folklore 34, 40–45 (2017).

177. Pub. L. 93–638, Jan. 4, 1975, 88 Stat. 2203, codified as amended at 25 U.S.C. § 5301 et seq.

178. Vine Deloria, Jr. and Clifford M. Lytle, *American Indians, American Justice* 111–116 (1983).

179. *United States v. Kagama*, 118 U.S. 375 (1886) (authorizing Congress to assert criminal jurisdiction over internal tribal matters).

180. Report of the Institute for Government Research, The Problems of Indian Administration (1928).

181. Wheeler-Howard Act, Act of June 18, 1934, 48 Stat. 984, codified at 25 U.S.C. §§ 5101 et seq.

182. Pub. L. 90–284, Title II, § 201, 82 Stat. 77 (1968), codified at 25 U.S.C. §§ 1301 et seq. See generally Matthew L. M. Fletcher, *Federal Indian Law* § 6.4 at 247–266 (2016).

183. 436 U.S. 49 (1978).

184. Catharine MacKinnon, Whose Culture? A Case Note on *Martinez v. Santa Clara Pueblo*, in *Feminism Unmodified* 63–69 (1987); Catharine MacKinnon, Martinez Revisited, in *The Indian Civil Rights Act at Forty* 27-38 (Kirsten A. Carpenter, Matthew L. M. Fletcher, and Angela R. Riley, eds. 2012).

185. Matthew L. M. Fletcher (with Alicia Ivory), Tribal Courts, the Indian Civil Rights Act, and Customary Law: Preliminary Data, MSU Legal Studies Research Paper No. 06-05 (2008), https://ssrn.com/abstract=1103474.

186. Wenona T. Singel, *Indian Tribes and Human Rights Accountability*, 49 San Diego L. Rev. 567 (2012) (collecting examples of criticism).

187. Brief of Andrea M. Seielstad as Amicus Curiae in Support of Petitioner, *Taveras v. Whitehouse*, __ U.S. __, 138 S. Ct. 1323 (2018) (No.17-429), 2017 WL 4857396.

188. Pub. L. 113-4, Title IX, § 904, Mar. 7, 2013, 127 Stat. 120, codified in relevant part at 25 U.S.C. § 1304.

189. Pub. L. 95–608, Nov. 8, 1978, 92 Stat. 3069, codified at 25 U.S.C. § 1901 et seq.

190. Brief Amicus Curiae of the Goldwater Institute in Support of Petitioner, *Taveras v. Whitehouse*, __ U.S. __, 138 S. Ct. 1323 (2018) (No.17-429), 2018 WL 1210848.

191. *Raphael v. Election Board*, No. 13-2189 (Grand Traverse Band Judiciary 2014), https://turtletalk.files.wordpress.com/2013/05/raphael-final-opinion.pdf.

192. 25 U.S.C. § 1302(a)(8).

193. The Deserted Boy, in 2 William Jones, *Ojibwa Texts* 745–763 (Truman Michaelson, ed. 1919).

194. Meghan Y. McCune, "It's a Question of Fairness": Fee-to-Trust and Opposition to Haudenosaunee Land Rights and Economic Development, in *Gambling on Authenticity: Gaming, the Noble Savage, and the Not-So-New Indian*, at 111 (Becca Gercken and Julie Pelletier, eds. 2018).

195. Brief for Citizens Equal Rights Foundation and Central New York Fair Business Association as Amici Curiae Supporting Petitioner, Washington v. United States, __ US __, 138 S. Ct. 1832 (2018) (No. 17-269), 2018 WL 1203453 [CERF Brief].

196. 31 U.S. 515 (1832).

197. Matthew L. M. Fletcher, *Federal Indian Law* § 2.3, at 37–45 (2016).

198. Fletcher, *supra* §§ 12.1, 12.2, and 12.4, at 505–516, 520–532.

199. 198 U.S. 371 (1905).

200. 207 U.S. 564 (1908).

201. CERF Brief, *supra* at 3.

202. CERF Brief, *supra* at 10.

203. CERF Brief, *supra* at 23.

204. CERF Brief, *supra* at 27.

205. E.g., Reid Peyton Chambers, *Implementing the Federal Trust Responsibility to Indians After President Nixon's 1970 Message to Congress on Indian Affairs: Reminiscences of Reid Peyton Chambers*, 53 Tulsa L. Rev. 395 (2018) (describing the work of the Department of the Interior's Office of the Solicitor in the 1970s in support of tribal interests).

206. CERF Brief, *supra* at 27.

207. CERF Brief, *supra* at 29.

208. CERF Brief, *supra* at 29–30.

209. The tribes did prevail in this case, with the Supreme Court affirming without opinion after a four-to-four tie vote on June 11, 2018.

210. Why Dogs Fight, and Why People are Envious, in 2 William Jones, *Ojibwa Texts* 755–757 (Truman Michaelson, ed. 1919).

211. Julie Turkewitz, *For Native Americans, a "Historic Moment" on the Path to Power at the Ballot Box*, New York Times, Jan. 4, 2018.

212. *Navajo Nation v. San Juan County*, 2017 WL 6547635 (D. Utah, Dec. 21, 2017) (remedial phase); *Navajo Nation v. San Juan County*, 266 F.Supp.3d 1341 (D. Utah) (voting rights phase). The appellate decision is reported at 929 F.3d 1270 (10th Cir. 2019).

213. The Petroglyph Blog, *San Juan County Citizens Facing Slavery and Racism*, Mar. 6, 2018.

214. Jennifer Denetdale, *The Navajo Long Walk: The Forced Navajo Exile* (2009).

215. 15 Stat. 667.

216. See Chapter 9.

217. Act of Nov. 2, 1921, c. 115, 42 Stat. 208, codified at 25 U.S.C. § 13.

218. Act of June 2, 1924, 43 Stat. 253, codified at 8 U.S.C. § 1401(b).

219. Wells is probably referring to the US Supreme Court's order in 1957 vacating a Utah Supreme Court decision in *Allen v. Merrell*, 305 P.3d 490 (Utah), that denied a Navajo Nation citizen's rights to vote in a state election. 353 U.S. 932 (1957).

220. Shawn Smallman, *Dangerous Spirits: The Windigo and History* (2014); Basil Johnston, *The Supernatural World of the Ojibway* 222 (1991); John Borrows, *Drawing Out Law: A Spirit's Guide* 223–224, 226 (2010); Linda LeGarde Grover, Windigo Presence in Selected Contemporary Ojibwe Prose and Poetry, in *Indigenous Voices Indigenous Symbols* 18, 18 (Rachael Selby ed., 2009).

221. E.g., Terry Anderson, *Sovereign Nations or Reservations: An Economic History of Reservations* (1995); Naomi Schaefer Riley, *The New Trail of Tears: How Washington Is Destroying Indians* (2016); Shawn E. Regan and Terry L. Anderson, *The Energy Wealth of Indian Nations*, 3 LSU J. Energy L. and Re-

sources 195 (2014). For a powerful and comprehensive critique of what I call privatization radicals, see Kristen A. Carpenter and Angela Riley, *Privatizing the Reservation?*, 71 Stan. L. Rev. 791 (2019).

222.ˋRegan and Anderson, *supra* at 195.

223. See Chapters 4 and 5.

224. Regan and Anderson, *supra* at 196.

225. See Chapter 9.

226. See Chapter 12.

227. See Chapter 5.

228. 25 U.S.C. § 177.

229. 25 U.S.C. § 5108.

230. 25 U.S.C. § 81.

231. 25 U.S.C. § 396.

232. Schafer Riley, *supra* at 14–15.

233. Pub. L. 92–203, Dec. 18, 1971, 85 Stat. 688, codified at 43 U.S.C. §§ 1601 et seq.

234. Regan and Anderson, *supra* at 212 and nn. 103–104, 213 and nn. 110–111.

235. Thomas Fiddler and James R. Stevens, *Killing The Shamen* 88–91 (1985).

236. The Legend of the Sleeping Bear, in John P. Coady, *The Legends and Story of the Michigan Indians* 2 (1993).

237. When Makwa Nowii Climbed Sleeping Bear Dunes, in Howard Webkamigad, *Ottawa Stories from the Springs* (anishinaabe dibaadjimowinan wodi gaa binjibaamigack wodi mookodjiwong e zhiniakaadek) 252–264 (2015).

238. *Bugenig v. Hoopa Valley Tribe*, 5 NICS App. 37 (Hoopa Valley Tribal Court of Appeals 1998).

239. *Bugenig v. Hoopa Valley Tribe*, 229 F.3d 1210 (9th Cir. 2000), rev'd 266 F.3d 1201 (9th Cir. 2001) (en banc), cert. denied, 535 U.S. 927 (2002).

240. The same panel of judges joined together in another case, argued the same day as the *Bugenig* case, involving tribal powers. In that case, Judge Gould's

opinion harshly condemned a tribal court judgment as violative of non-Indian rights. *Bird v. Glacier Electric Cooperative, Inc.*, 255 F.3d 1136 (9th Cir. 2001). Professor Bob Clinton slammed the court's decision there, picking apart the reasoning of the *Bird* panel decision line by line. Robert N. Clinton, *Comity and Colonialism: The Federal Courts' Frustration of Federal—Tribal Cooperation*, 36 Ariz. St. L.J. 1, 51–58 (2004).

241. *Bugenig*, 229 F.3d at 1222.

242. Old Man Mashos, in 2 William Jones, *Ojibwa Texts* 179–189 (Truman Michaelson, ed. 1919).

243. David E. Wilkins, *The Red Prophet: The Punishing Intellectualism of Vine Deloria, Jr.* (2018).

244. For more on this mythology, see Chapter 1.

245. Gordon Wood, *Federalism from the Ground Up*, 78 U. Chi. L. Rev. 705, 706 (2011) (reviewing Alison L. LaCroix, *The Ideological Origins of American Federalism* (2010)).

246. *Id.* at 705–706 (citing 1 HR Cong. Res. 331, 100th Cong., 2d Sess. (Oct 21, 1988), in 102 Stat. 4932; Contributions of the Iroquois Confederacy Indian Nations – Recognizing Contributions to the United States, Iroquois Confederacy of Nations, S. Cong. Res. 76, 100th Cong., 2d Sess. (Sept. 16, 1987), in 134 Cong. Rec. S 29528 (Oct 7, 1988)).

247. LaCroix's quietly devastating rebuttal to Wood on the merits of the core of her book does not even mention the Haudenosaunee influence theory; she simply didn't need to say anything. Alison L. LaCroix, *Rhetoric and Reality in Early American Legal History: A Reply to Gordon Wood*, 78 U. Chi. L. Rev. 733 (2011).

248. Erik M. Jensen, *The Harvard Law Review and the Iroquois Influence Thesis*, 6 Brit. J. Am. Legal Stud. 22 (2017).

249. Jensen, *supra* at 226–227.

250. Jensen, *supra* at 227, 237, 238.

251. Jensen, *supra* at 228.

252. Erik M. Jensen, *The Imaginary Connection Between the Great Law of Peace and the United States Constitution: A Reply to Professor Schaaf*, 15 Am. Indian L. Rev. 295 (1991).

253. Jensen, *supra* at 230.

254. Jensen, *supra* at 231.

255. Jensen, *supra* at 236.

256. Jensen, *supra* at 236 (quoting Barbara A. Mann, Haudensee (Iroquois) League, origin date, entry in *Encyclopedia of the Haudenosaunee (Iroquois Confederacy)* 152 (Bruce Elliott Johansen and Barbara Alice Mann, eds., 2000)).

257. Jensen, *supra* at 236.

258. Jensen, *supra* at 236.

259. Old Toad-Woman Steals a Child, in 2 William Jones, *Ojibwa Texts* 427–441 (Truman Michaelson, ed. 1919); The Toad Woman, in John C. Wright, *The Crooked Tree: Indian Legends of Northern Michigan* 53–59 (1915).

260. Indian Child Welfare Program, Hearings before the Subcommittee on Indian Affairs of the Senate Committee on Interior and Insular Affairs, 93d Cong., 2d Sess., 3 (statement of William Byler), cited in Mississippi Band of Choctaw *Indians v. Holyfield*, 490 US 30, 32–33 (1989). See also 25 U.S.C. 1901(4) (finding that "an alarmingly high percentage of Indian families are broken up by the removal, often unwarranted, of their children from them by non-tribal public and private agencies and that an alarmingly high percentage of such children are placed in non-Indian foster and adoptive homes and institutions").

261. 25 U.S.C. § 1912(b).

262. 25 U.S.C. § 1912(a).

263. *Id.*

264. 25 U.S.C. § 1911(a).

265. 25 U.S.C. § 1911(b).

266. 25 U.S.C. § 1912(f).

267. Brief of Casey Family Programs et al., *Adoptive Couple v. Baby Girl*, 570 U.S. 637 (2013) (No. 12-399), 2018 WL 1279468.

268. The Magic Flight, in William Jones, *Ojibwa Tales from the North Shore of Lake Superior*, 29:113 J. Am. Folklore 368, 379–380 (1916); The Magic Flight, in Alanson Skinner, *Plains Ojibwa Tales*, 32:124 J. Am. Folklore 280,

291–292 (1919). Compare this to the story of the rolling head, a Cheyenne story, told in Tommy Orange's novel *There There* (2018).

269. The Orphans and Mashos, in 2 William Jones, *Ojibwa Texts* 45–103 (Truman Michaelson, ed. 1919).

270. Old Man Mashos, in 2 William Jones, *Ojibwa Texts* 179–191 (Truman Michaelson, ed. 1919); End of a Mashos Story, in William Jones, *Ojibwa Tales from the North Shore of Lake Superior*, 29:113 J. Am. Folklore 368, 377 (1916). See also Chapter 16.

271. The Tower, *Adventure Time*, season 6, episode 4 (2014).

272. The Vault, *Adventure Time*, season 5, episode 34 (2013).

273. The Creeps, *Adventure Time*, season 3, episode 12 (2011).

ANISHINAABE TERMS

aadizookaan – story

Aakodewin – bravery

aandeg – crow

aaniin – hello or welcome

ajidamoo – squirrel

Ajijaak Dodem – crane clan

Andahaunahquodishkung – moose

Animikii Binesiwaag – Thunderbirds

Animikiiwaag – Thunderbird

Anishinaabemowin – Anishinaabe language

Anishinaabewaki – the world of the Anishinaabe; the Great Lakes

Benodjehn – a baby

Bineshinh Dodem – bird clan

binewaag – partridges

boozhoo – welcome, greetings, hello, hi

chmookmon – Americans, literally "long knife"

dabazi – duck

Debwewin – truth

Dibaadenizowin – humility

dodem – clan

doodeminaan – clans

gaagaai – raven

Gagige Inaakonige – eternal natural law

giigoon – fish

Giigoon Dodem – fish clan

Gwekowaadiziwin – honesty

inaakonigewin – law

inini – man

ininiwaag – men

jeebikana – ghost road

jeebiwaag – ghosts

jeebiziibi – the river of death

jiimaan – canoe

kwe – woman

Maang Dodem – loon clan

maanwaag – loons

mai'ingan – wolf

makwaag – bears

Manaadjitowaawin – respect

manidowaag – the spirits

manitou – spirit

matchimanidowaag – bad spirits or monsters

Meshike Dodem – turtle clan

Michibizhii – underwater panther monster

Michilimackinac – Turtle Island

migizi – eagle

miigwetch – thank you

Mino-Bimaadiziwin – the act of living a good life

Miskwaadesi – painted turtle

Mishomis – grandfather

mooz – moose

mukwa – bear

Mukwa Dodem – bear clan

namé – sturgeon

Nanaboozhoo – Anishinaabe trickster god

Nibwaakaawin – wisdom

Niimaamaa – mother

Niizhwaaswii Mishomis – Seven Grandfather teachings

nigig – otter

Nokomis – grandmother

Nokomis Kinoomaagewinawaan – Seven Grandmother teachings

ode'imin – strawberry

ogaa – walleye

ogema – leader

ogemaag – leaders

Onaabani-giizis – Hard Crust on the Snow Moon, or March

Pagonekiishig – four concentric circles in the sky

Pimaatiziwin – create the good life

semaa – tobacco

tiginaagan – cradleboard

Waabizheshi dodem – marten clan

waawaashkeshi – deer

Waawaashkeshi Dodem – deer clan

Wabanaki – dawn land

Waganakising – the traditional name for an important village affiliated with the Little Traverse Bay Bands of Odawa Indians

Wazhashk – muskrat

wemitigosh – the French, literally "men who wave sticks"

windigo – horrific mystical creature

zaaga'igan – lake

Zaagidwin love

Zhaganash – the British, literally meaning "people who rise from the mist"; also an old word for "weapon"

INDEX

ABOUT THE AUTHOR

Matthew L.M. Fletcher, a member of the Grand Traverse Band, is Professor of Law at Michigan State University College of Law and Director of the Indigenous Law and Policy Center. He sits as the Chief Justice of the Poarch Band of Creek Indians Supreme Court and also sits as an appellate judge for the Grand Traverse Band of Ottawa and Chippewa Indians, the Hoopa Valley Tribe, the Mashpee Wampanoag Tribe, the Match-E-Be-Nash-She-Wish Band of Pottawatomi Indians, the Pokagon Band of Potawatomi Indians, the Nottawaseppi Huron Band of Potawatomi Indians, the Rincon Band of Luiseño Indians, the Santee Sioux Tribe of Nebraska, and the Tulalip Tribes. In addition to writing *Federal Indian Law* and *Principles of Federal Indian Law*, Fletcher has co-authored numerous publications, and is the primary editor and author of the leading law blog on American Indian law and policy, "Turtle Talk," http://turtletalk.wordpress.com/.